Design
Principles

Color ◆ Form ◆ Styles

Ellen Cheever, CMKBD, ASID

Professional Resource Library

About The National Kitchen & Bath Association

As the only non-profit trade association dedicated exclusively to the kitchen and bath industry, the National Kitchen & Bath Association (NKBA) is the leading source of information and education for all professionals in the field.

NKBA's mission is to enhance member success and excellence by promoting professionalism and ethical business practices, and by providing leadership and direction for the kitchen and bath industry.

A non-profit trade association with more than 25,000 members in North America and overseas, it has provided valuable resources for industry professionals for more than forty years. Its members are the finest professionals in the kitchen and bath industry.

NKBA has pioneered innovative industry research, developed effective business management tools, and set groundbreaking standards for safe, functional and comfortable design of kitchens and baths.

NKBA provides a unique, one-stop resource for professional reference materials, seminars and workshops, distance learning opportunities, marketing assistance, design competitions, consumer referrals, job and internship opportunities and opportunities for volunteer leadership activities.

Recognized as the kitchen and bath industry's education and information leader, NKBA provides development opportunities and continuing education for all levels of professionals. More than 100 courses, as well as a certification program with three internationally recognized levels, help kitchen and bath professionals raise the bar for excellence.

For students entering the industry, NKBA offers Supported and Endorsed Programs, which provide NKBA-approved curriculum at more than 47 learning institutions throughout North America.

NKBA helps members and other industry professionals stay on the cutting-edge of an ever-changing field through the Association's Kitchen/Bath Industry Show, one of the largest trade shows in the country.

NKBA offers membership in four different categories: Industry, Associate, Student and Honorary. Industry memberships are broken into eleven different industry segments. For more information, visit NKBA at www.nkba.org.

THANK YOU TO OUR SPONSORS

The National Kitchen & Bath Association recognizes with gratitude the following companies who generously helped to fund the creation of this industry resource.

PATRONS

www.americanwoodmark.com

www.kohler.com

BENEFACTORS

www.monogram.com

www.subzero.com www.wolfappliance.com

CONTRIBUTOR

www.groheamerica.com

SUPPORTERS

www.nyloft.net

SHOW SH HOUSE.
by MOEN

www.showhouse.moen.com

TOTO®

www.totousa.com

DONORS

Rev-A-Shelf | Viking Range Corp. | Whirlpool Corp.

This book is intended for professional use by residential kitchen and bath designers. The procedures and advice herein have been shown to be appropriate for the applications described; however, no warranty (expressed or implied) is intended or given. Moreover, the user of this book is cautioned to be familiar with and to adhere to all manufacturers' planning, installation and use/care instructions. In addition, the user is urged to become familiar with and adhere to all applicable local, state and federal building codes, licensing and legislation requirements governing the user's ability to perform all tasks associated with design and installation standards, and to collaborate with licensed practitioners who offer professional services in the technical areas of mechanical, electrical and load bearing design as required for regulatory approval, as well as health and safety regulations.

Information about this book and other association programs
and publications may be obtained from the
National Kitchen & Bath Association
687 Willow Grove Street, Hackettstown, New Jersey 07840
Phone (800) 843-6522
www.nkba.org

ISBN 1-887127-53-4

First Edition 2006

Illustrations by: Jerry Germer and Karen Dorion

Top cover photo courtesy Showcase/V6B Design Group, Vancouver, British Columbia
Bottom cover photo courtesy Merrie Fredericks, CKD, CBD – Landsdowne, PA

Published on behalf of NKBA by Fry Communications, Irvine, CA

Peer Reviewers

Timothy Aden, CMKBD	Jim Krengel, CMKBD
Julia Beamish, Ph.D, CKE	Chris LaSpada, CPA
Leonard V. Casey	Elaine Lockard
Ellen Cheever, CMKBD, ASID	Phyllis Markussen, Ed.D, CKE, CBE
Hank Darlington	Chris J Murphy, CKD, CBD, CKBI
Dee David, CKD, CBD	David Newton, CMKBD
Peggy Deras, CKD, CID	Roberta Null, Ph.D
Kimball Derrick, CKD	Michael J Palkowitsch, CMKBD
Tim DiGuardi	Paul Pankow, CKBI
Kathleen Donohue, CMKBD	Jack Parks
Gretchen L. Edwards, CMKBD	Kathleen R. Parrott, Ph.D, CKE
JoAnn Emmel, Ph.D	Al Pattison,CMKBD
Jerry Germer	Les Petrie, CMKBD
Pietro A. Giorgi, Sr., CMKBD	Becky Sue Rajala, CKD
Tom Giorgi	Betty L. Ravnik, CKD, CBD
Jerome Hankins, CKD	Robert Schaefer
Spencer Hinkle, CKD	Klaudia Spivey, CMKBD
Max Isley, CMKBD	Kelly Stewart, CMKBD
Mark Karas, CMKBD	Tom Trzcinski, CMKBD
Martha Kerr, CMKBD	Stephanie Witt, CMKBD

TABLE OF CONTENTS

INTRODUCTION. . . . . **xi**

    A Brief History of the Kitchen xii

    A Brief History of the Bathroom. xvii

CHAPTER 1 – The Basics of Beauty. **1**

    Developing Style 3

    Creativity: Is It a Natural Gift?. 3

    A Definition of Good Design. 4

        A Unified Look   4

        A Timeless Look   7

CHAPTER 2 – Personalizing the Design. **11**

    Specific Kitchen or Bathroom Questions. 12

    Product Specifications 13

    Existing Construction 13

    Design Information. 13

    Properly Document Information. 14

    Final Design Considerations 14

CHAPTER 3 – The Elements of Design **15**

    Line 15

        Horizontal Line   16

        Vertical Line   19

        Curved Line   21

        Diagonal Line   23

    Combining Lines 26

    Shape 26

    Identifying Pattern Preference. 35

        Structural   36

        Naturalistic   38

        Stylized   40

        Geometric   42

        Abstract   44

    Space and Form 46

        Pyramid   46

        "H" Form   46

        Step Ladder   46

    Texture. 50

    Color 55

Hue 55

Color Categories. 56

    Attributes   59

    Chroma   59

    Value   60

Harmony 62

    Monochromatic   63

    Analogous   65

    Analogous with a Complementary Accent   66

    Triad   67

    Complementary   68

    Neutral   70

Color and Its Emotional Impact. 72

    Yellow   72

    Green   72

    Blue   72

    Purple   73

    Reds and Pinks   73

    Oranges and Browns   73

Transforming Space with Color. 74

Importance of Color. 75

CHAPTER 4 – The Principles of Design. 76

Balance. 76

    Symmetrical Balance   76

    Asymmetrical Balance   80

    Radial   83

Continuity/Rhythm. 84

    Repetitive   84

    Alternation   87

    Progression   90

    Domination   93

Emphasis 93

    Area Emphasis   93

    Theme Emphasis   98

Conclusion 100

CHAPTER 5 – Creating a Theme Environment **101**

    Establishing a Theme for a Kitchen or Bathroom Project. 101

    Theme Styling Terminology 102

    Eclectic Design 103

    Enhancing a New Kitchen or Bathroom with Old Objects 103

    Placing a New Kitchen or Bathroom within an Old Setting 103

    The Collector's Mix. 104

    The Signature Element 104

    Architectural History Review 104

        Classicism   104

        Gothic   105

        Renaissance   105

    Theme Kitchens and Bathrooms. 108

        American Classic Rustic   109

        American Shaker   113

        Arts and Crafts   116

        Rustic Americana   121

        American Classic Formal   124

        American Traditional   128

        Victorian   132

        European Classic Rustic   136

        French Country   141

        Italian Tuscan   147

        Scandinavian Country   151

        European Classic Formal   152

    Diversity of 21st Century Contemporary Design. 156

        Artisan Crafted   158

        East Meets West   166

        Urban Contemporary   172

        Mid-Century Modernism   182

    A Closing Comment. 190

LIST OF PHOTOS. **193**

LIST OF ILLUSTRATIONS **195**

INDEX. **196**

INTRODUCTION

AESTHETIC DESIGN IS AS IMPORTANT AS FUNCTIONAL SPACE PLANNING IN KITCHENS AND BATHROOMS

The consumer's definition of good design in residential kitchen and bath planning places equal importance on function and beauty.

- Consumers expect a kitchen to work as well as it looks. One aspect of the plan is not "given up" for the other.

- Consumers pride themselves in planning their own kitchen or bath; however, they expect the kitchen/bath specialist to help them create a personalized "one-of-a-kind" space.

- Consumers who specify luxury products as well as those on a more modest budget are interested in good style. Their appreciation of style has grown because consumers are exposed to well-designed home products created by recognized artists or home fashion experts in mass retail stores, on television home decorating shows and on the internet.

To meet this professional challenge and provide design excellence, both experienced and novice designers must expand their planning expertise to encompass the elements and principles of design. This requires both academic study, as well as the ability to think beyond our industry standard of covering the walls with well-engineered cabinets and highly functional, well-made manufactured materials.

This volume of the *Professional Resource Library* explains the elements and principles of design and applies them to actual kitchen and bath situations, enabling you to clearly understand how to apply the tools of design to your daily business practice.

A BRIEF HISTORY OF THE KITCHEN

Long ago, a kitchen was in a separate building apart from the home to protect the family's dwelling from fires. The kitchen slowly became attached to the dwelling and, in Colonial days, was the "heart of the home" with the open flame from the fireplace used to warm the family as well as cook the food.

Figure 1.1 *An Historical Kitchen*
The kitchen of the Rundlett-May House (1807) in Portsmouth, New Hampshire, features an enclosed fireplace—an early forerunner of the modern kitchen stove. (Photograph by David Bohl, Courtesy of the Society of Preservation of New England Antiquities)

The idea of a well-planned, well-designed kitchen was first talked about in the 1920s when Hoosier cabinets were introduced by the Hoosier Company, and Cornell University began research on functional planning. However, the room still remained a workroom, where function and ease of cleaning were the only consideration.

Figure 1.2 *1940s Kitchen*
Kitchens of the 1940s were a mecca of mass production and easy-to-clean surfaces. (Courtesy of Kohler Company)

Immediately following World War II, several leading Midwestern and Eastern cabinet companies introduced color for the cabinetry, as well as decorative hardware and interesting accent cabinet pieces. Built-in appliances were introduced in the late 1950s and 1960s, as well. These avant-garde kitchens were highly touted in fashion magazines such as *Town & Country* and *Vogue*, as well as home design shelter publications.

Figure 1.3 *1960s Kitchen*
In the 1960s wood became the material of choice for cabinetry, and built-in cabinets were introduced. (Courtesy of Wood-Mode Inc.)

In the 1970s, a startling new concept was introduced in several well-respected shelter magazines—the idea of the "Great Room." Walls were torn down between the kitchen and adjacent living spaces, bringing the kitchen out of the "dungeon" category, into serving a role as part of the family public space. The concept of the Great Room brought mass appeal to the idea of a decorated kitchen—one that was attractive to look at, as well as functional to work in.

The concept of an aesthetically pleasing kitchen grew in importance throughout the 1970s, 1980s and into the 1990s as the English "bespoke" idea of an "unfitted kitchen" was coupled with the consumer's interest in highly stylized environments attempting to recreate the warmth of a sun-drenched villa in Tuscany, or a cozy Colonial cottage in New England. Architectural details from these historic settings became more and more popular for consumers planning kitchens that were becoming center stage in their homes.

Figure 1.4 *Kitchens from Today – Traditional*
A traditional kitchen with finely crafted Old World design details is a popular look for kitchens today. (Courtesy of Bryan Reiss, CKD, CBD and Scott Stultz and co-designers Peter Deane and Kelly Stewart, CMKBD – Stamford, Connecticut)

The interest in such beautiful spaces continues today. As a kitchen specialist, you may be asked to plan a room that has a European influenced style, or one that is harmonious and calming, inspired by a Pacific Rim interior. With all these design requests, your ability to use the elements and principles of good design will add great value to your functional space planning solutions.

Figure 1.5 *Kitchens from Today – Contemporary*
Contemporary kitchens today combine function and beauty. In this example, simple veneer cabinets are highlighted with an oversized cabinet pull. Stainless steel and polished black granite are contrasted with a decorative backsplash featuring a black tile decorative piece. (Courtesy of George Fakhoury – West Paterson, New Jersey. Photography by Peter Rymwid.)

A BRIEF HISTORY
OF THE BATHROOM

Although luxury homes featured indoor bathrooms in the late 1800s, it was not until the 1920s that building codes began mandating indoor plumbing for all residences. These new laws paid little attention to the way the bathroom looked because it was perceived simply as a utilitarian space. For the typical bathroom, few choices existed for fixture colors or fitting finishes. The only concern was how to squeeze three basic white fixtures in the smallest space possible.

Figure 1.6 *Historical Plumbing* Providing a safe indoor supply of water was the primary concern of early planners. (Courtesy of Kohler Company)

Although many builders, designers and architects overlooked the potential beauty of the bathroom, American film makers and trendsetters realized how lovely a bathroom could be. Sets in Hollywood movies during the 1920s and 1930s suggested the potential beauty of the bathroom. Major manufacturers extended their product lines and introduced color. In 1929, the New York Metropolitan Museum of Art featured an exhibit devoted to the artistic qualities of the bathroom.

Figure 1.7 *Historical Bathroom*
An early Kohler advertisement celebrates color in the bathroom. (Courtesy of Kohler Company)

The fantasies of dream-makers all those years ago are the reality for well-planned bathrooms today. The bathroom is no longer a room reserved for simple personal hygiene. Today, people spend more time in the space. Some gather in a family group to enjoy the therapeutic pleasure of a hydromassage bath; others use the bathroom as a secluded spot away from hectic family and job responsibilities.

As a bathroom specialist, you may be asked to plan part of a major master bedroom suite, or a bathroom that is a separate, compartmentalized, hard-working room. Your client may request a dramatic powder room reserved for guests, or a shower space squeezed off the utility room or outdoor cabana.

In all of these situations, your ability to use the elements and principles of good design adds great value to your functional space planning solution.

Figure 1.8 *Bathrooms from Today*
A modern master bathroom retreat uses a tambour-type cabinet arrangement to provide concealed storage at the vanity in a room with a soft monochromatic color scheme featuring naturalistic materials. (Courtesy of Greg Rawson, CKD, CBD – Muncie, Indiana)

CHAPTER 1: The Basics Of Beauty: Developing Skill, Expanding Creativity And Appreciating Style

The primary focus of this volume is on the physical appearance of the kitchen and bathroom. It details how to apply the academic elements and principles of design to specific kitchen and bathroom situations. While references to kitchen layouts, types of equipment and various materials are made, the major thrust of this volume is how the kitchen or bath visually presents itself to the viewer enjoying the space.

People oftentimes mistakenly believe that designers have a "knack" —a natural talent—for design. While a natural affinity—a discerning eye—is definitely part of a good designer's ability, leaders in our industry, as well as educators in the field of interior design or space planning, all agree that understanding and applying accepted guidelines—is the foundation of an individual's basic skill set. These guidelines are known as the elements and principles of design.

Experience within the field leads to the development of a sense of style. And a sense of style is much more difficult to categorize than a rule-based formula.

The individual's ability to creatively think beyond the boundaries of accepted ideas leads to individual, unique solutions appropriate for each client's home.

Therefore, learning the rules—the elements and principles of design—always comes first. Mastering these guidelines, combined with keen observation and experience, increases the designer's ability to think beyond the ordinary.

SKILL IS THE EXECUTOR OF A DESIGN PROGRAM. SKILL IDENTIFIES ACCEPTABLE CHOICES.

The designer's style directs the effort—by this, we mean style is the designer's ability to select one choice from several acceptable alternatives.

Figure 1.9 *The Basics of Beauty*

At the Kohler Design Center, a setting created by designer Oscar Shamaniam, titled "Le Bain Parc Monseau," demonstrates a beautiful bathroom—skillfully created—with a great sense of style. The designer's skill led him to alternate 12" x 12" black-and-white marble tiles on the floor combined with a symmetrically balanced vanity wall. The designer's style introduced the wood paneling in a bathroom bringing the sense of library into this personal bathing space. Additionally, it is the designer's style that added the framed marble on the floor to differentiate the area serving the water closet and tub from that reserved for the vanity. (Courtesy of Kohler Company)

IT'S EASY TO UNDERSTAND SKILL— BUT HOW DO YOU DEVELOP YOUR STYLE?

Developing a design style takes experience based on observation. The best way to begin is to become more visually aware of good design, which is around you all the time.

- Look at a garden—it is probably symmetrically balanced.

- When you are watching television, study the commercials. The clothes are probably coordinated with the background set. The lighting may play a key part in establishing a focal point.

- Stop and admire window displays in storefronts. The balance, rhythm and color combinations are oftentimes just the beginning of these highly styled vignettes.

To gather examples of good design in your industry:

- Study kitchen and bathroom designs in consumer and trade magazines, noting how the details of the spaces are woven together. Don't stop there—tear out pages that feature great examples and begin your own "idea library."

- Visit showrooms. Evaluate how the spaces are laid out and the products combined. Look closely for small design detailing. By the way, in addition to showrooms, invest in your own education by purchasing good books featuring kitchen design and attending trade shows where product is displayed. You can learn about design, from both a skill and style standpoint—as well as product features and benefits—in these settings created by masterful merchandisers.

CREATIVITY: IS IT A NATURAL GIFT? – OR CAN IT BE LEARNED?

As Kathleen Donohue, CMKBD, a noted Northwestern designer, once said,

"The prevailing opinion in our society is that creativity and a flair for design are inherent abilities that either one has or does not have. Because creativity is so often (and I firmly believe incorrectly) regarded as a subjective ability that cannot be measured quantitatively, kitchen and bath specialists tend to be at their least confident when a client asks about color, fabric or specific styles appropriate to the kitchen, which has been carefully created from a functional standpoint by the designer."

Designers worry because they are not sure if they are "creative." Will their recommendations be based simply on their personal taste?

3

And so, they come across as tentative and insecure when making recommendations about the materials, patterns and architectural detailing that truly round out their design work.

For the kitchen and bathroom designer, creativity can best be defined as presenting a common solution in an unusual yet practical way. Winners in our industry understand the true definition of creativity: "Creativity is the emergence of something new which is relative, useful or important."

The word "new" is not to be construed as something never in existence before; rather, "new" generally means an accumulation of knowledge coming together in a unique manner to supply an answer not reached before, or a solution not tried in the past. Therefore, your ability to be creative is not limited to a natural talent allowing you to do something never conceived before, but rather it is your dedication to continually search for variations in the way you treat space.

The true foundation of creativity is diligence, perseverance and dedication. As Pablo Picasso once said, "There are painters who transform the sun into a yellow spot, but there are others, who with the help of their art and their intelligence, transform a yellow spot into the sun." George Bernard Shaw shared another truism when he said, "Few people think more than two or three times a year. I've made an international reputation for myself by thinking once or twice a week."

Creativity is a human potential of all individuals. As you step beyond the basics of kitchen and bath functional planning, learning the elements and principles of design and the basic themes appropriate for creating stylized rooms, you are developing a skill level which will lead to increasing your creative thinking abilities—and along the way, your self-confidence as well.

A DEFINITION OF GOOD DESIGN

After establishing the difference between learned skill, acquired style, and emancipated creativity, it is still worthwhile pondering the question, "What is the simplest definition of 'good design'?"

A Unified Look

Masters in our field agree that the most important part of any room is that it has a "unified look." The key to a unified look is how each individual part of the room relates to the others. Unity of design does not mean the entire room must be the same; i.e., the same color, the same style, the same material. Far from it. Indeed, eclectic combinations of unusual and dissimilar items are very popular today.

Rather, "unity of design" means that all dissimilar items or elements of the space are visually tied together in an organized, logical, balanced—yet interesting way. Here, again, is where knowing the rules—the elements and principles of design—will start the newcomer down the path towards success and reinvigorate a veteran in our industry who is looking for ways to refresh his/her approach to kitchen planning.

Figure 1.10 *The Basics of Beauty: A Unified Kitchen*
One design approach to creating unity is to combine different materials in blocks of space. The dark wood and stainless steel of the storage area is continued in dark wood panels surrounded by stainless steel trim in the island. (Courtesy of Downsview Kitchens)

Figure 1.11 *The Basics of Beauty: A Unified Bathroom*
The textured stone material anchors this bathroom space by its use on major horizontal and vertical surfaces. The horizontal tile stripe, length of mirror and reflectance (and neutrality) of the glass block make this both a unified and visually interesting space. (Courtesy of Arthur Krikor Halajian, CKD – San Rafael, California. Photography by Rusty Reniers)

A Timeless Look

The second "gold" standard of good design is that it stands the test of time. Experienced designers avoid fads and turn a skeptical eye on what is currently defined as fashionable.

They concentrate on proven style and solid quality, which is based on the appropriateness and durability of the design solutions and products incorporated in the room.

When evaluating a proposed solution or material for a major element in the room, ask yourself, "Will this be considered beautiful five years from now?" If you think not, you may want to try a different, more neutral approach for this long-lasting area. To add sparkle to such a cautious approach to design, specify bold patterns or colors — or unique materials for surfaces that are easily changed over the life expectancy of the room.

Figure 1.12 *The Basics of Beauty: Highly Stylized Kitchen*
This kitchen is a beautiful Old World setting. Such a highly stylistic design works well for clients who would enjoy this theme throughout their home. (Courtesy of Beverly Adams, CMKBD – Denver, Colorado)

Figure 1.13 *The Basics of Beauty: A Timeless Look*
The same designer demonstrates her high level of design diversity and abilities in creating this more Transitional kitchen that will stand the design test of time criteria very well. (Courtesy of Beverly Adams, CMKBD – Denver, Colorado)

Figure 1.14 *The Basics of Beauty: Tailored Timeless Design*
Another example of timeless design is presented in this
white kitchen. An understated combination of naturalistic
patterned surfaces is accented by Mid-Century Modern
furniture. (Courtesy of Eric Lieberknecht, Washington, D.C.
Photography by John Umberger Photography)

CHAPTER 2: Personalizing the Design

Top-notch designers strive to make the kitchens or bathrooms they create reflect the client's interests and preferences. Unfortunately, it is not uncommon to see a series of projects created by a designer that all have the same look to them. But the true professional will design each project so it is an individual, personal expression of the client.

To accomplish this, the designer must first spend more time listening than talking. Interior design professionals call this "the program phase" of the design process. Quite simply put—the first thing you must do is gather information. Using your own information gathering system, or the survey form developed by the National Kitchen & Bath Association, wise designers ask a series of preplanned questions and take careful note of the clients' answers in an organized fashion.

During this information gathering stage it is not appropriate to be focused on solutions. Rather, it is time to learn what the client likes and dislikes about their existing room, and what their dreams and hopes are for their new kitchen or bath. It is also critical to establish the budget for the project.

The information you gather should be divided into the following categories:

- General client information.

- Identify the budget for the project. (Knowing the financial limitations is as important as knowing their favorite color.)

- Ask about the time frame. If deadlines exist for the completion of the project, this may restrict the proposed list of products.

- Find out who are the key decision makers. Is there an interior designer involved, an architect or other key individuals who will be part of the decision-making process?

Of foremost importance is understanding the budget constraints, often overlooked by design professionals as a key element of their practice. However, the best in our business get a good sense of what the budget is before they begin the planning process.

TIPS FROM THE PROS:
HOW TO TALK ABOUT THE BUDGET WITH YOUR CLIENT

- *"The first thing I do when interviewing a client in the showroom or beginning a presentation is to give them choices. I want them to feel that even though I am in control of the design, they're in control of the budget. I'm not just a salesperson trying to push the price as high as I can. A client said to me the other day, 'Well, I do have a budget.' I said, 'Everybody has a budget, it's just some budgets are bigger than others.' My clients know I respect their budget and my industry knowledge will help them invest their money wisely."* (A designer in Connecticut)

- *"We usually discuss the budget right from the beginning and make it clear we put it at the top of our list of 'needs'. Just as more storage in a kitchen or a particular type of counter surface in the bath is a 'need', we tell our clients the budget should be at the top of that list as well."* (A designer in Georgia)

- *"I usually ask the client to give me an 'investment' price, rather than a 'budget' price."* (A designer in Colorado)

- *"If we've selected a cabinet line, and the dollar amount for those cabinets isn't within the client's range, I show them alternative options: whether it's a less expensive door or a more modestly priced finish option. I try to show them ways to keep the same design, but price it out for less."* (A designer in California)

SPECIFIC KITCHEN OR BATHROOM QUESTIONS

Following the general information, you'll want to ask specific questions about how the kitchen or bath is used. This is how a designer zeroes in on ways to personalize the space. For example, the kitchen designed strictly for adults who really do not cook at home allows far more latitude in product specifications than does a space that will be used by a busy family with three active teenagers who cook day in and day out. And an infrequently used powder room is planned differently than a hall bathroom used by the entire family.

In addition to asking specific questions about the kitchen and bath, pay close attention to how this room relates to adjacent spaces.

- Is the kitchen part of a general great room in the public areas of the home? It must be integrated with these other living spaces.

- Is the kitchen a walled-off space located between the living and formal dining rooms? Continuity between the various rooms may not be as important to the homeowners.

- Is it next to a family room or a breakfast nook? Such a room arrangement may let you combine the spaces into an open multi-purpose area. When it is next to the family room much more attention will be paid to the style details of this space because it must look like a living space as much as it does a kitchen.

PRODUCT SPECIFICATIONS

Next, you will focus on specific products—does the client need a built-in oven, or a freestanding 60-inch professional range? Is a bathing pool their dream—or, a spa-like jetted tub for two high on their priority list?

Noting all the client's preferences is a starting point—this is where you begin to personalize the space. You may, at a later date, need, or wish, to offer alternatives to the homeowner. But, the place to start is at the beginning: by listening more than talking.

EXISTING CONSTRUCTION

You will take note of construction constraints that may affect your design recommendations, as well as architectural or mechanical elements of the space that you must work with as you create your aesthetic design solution. (See the NKBA's *Kitchen Planning, Residential Construction* and *Kitchen & Bath Systems* books for details.)

DESIGN INFORMATION

The color and design specifics gathered help the designer personalize space for that client.

A good time to share your portfolio with the prospective client is as you begin asking color and design questions. By using perspectives of completed kitchens/bathrooms, or photographs of actual projects, you can show the client what different styles look like.

An idea book of pictures cut from magazines and divided by various themes and room layout possibilities is an excellent visual tool to help you describe design solutions. Oftentimes, consumers have pictures they have carefully saved over the years that reflect their wants and desires for the new room. Ask the client to show you pictures they have collected as well. Look carefully at the pictures and ask the client, "What is it about this picture that you like?" Be sure to clarify between functional preferences and stylistic ones.

PROPERLY DOCUMENT THE INFORMATION YOU GATHER

Take good notes, making a copy for your file as well. Many designers take digital photographs of the house exterior, the room under discussion and adjacent living spaces at the home survey appointment. This visual reference helps you study the details of the client's home as you begin the planning and personalization process back at your office.

FINAL DESIGN CONSIDERATIONS

When you complete the client survey in this manner, you will have carefully noted and cataloged the project limitations, client needs and the product requests. You will be able to determine how to take the necessary centers of activity in the kitchen or bathroom and combine them so that they form a well-organized room within the construction limitations and budget constraints of the project.

After you complete the conceptual space layout, you will use the intangible design guides, the rules and tools of the design trade, to create an aesthetically pleasing project as well.

CHAPTER 3: The Elements of Design

An understanding of the elements and principles of design allows you to find the best solution for a space. The elements are the tools designers work with. The principles guide designers in the use of those tools. Familiarize yourself with the elements, or tools, and then follow the design principles to create a total environment.

The elements of design are:

- Line

- Shape

- Space

- Form

- Texture

- Color

The principles of design (discussed more thoroughly in Chapter 4) include:

- Balance

- Rhythm

- Emphasis

LINE

Lines are the simplest shapes. Lines can evoke an emotional response and have the ability to stretch or shrink space visually. The section on shapes includes specific examples and illustrations.

A design rarely features just one type of line. Many types of lines are used in most spaces. However, there is generally a predominance of one type of line that contributes to the overall feeling of the space. You will see examples of such combinations as we study each type of line and shape.

Horizontal Line

Horizontal lines are the most stable of all line forms. The eye travels along the horizontal line, widening the area or object viewed. Horizontal lines feel calm and suggest rest and relaxation.

Wide horizontal lines that contrast strongly with background surfaces divide the overall elevation into alternating segments. Such a horizontal division works well to visually re-adjust the height in a room. For example, introduce a horizontal line about 12 inches below the ceiling by installing a decorative molding. A patterned surface can end just below the molding and the wall above the molding can be painted to match the ceiling. This tactic ties the upper 12 inches of the wall to the ceiling and visually lowers that ceiling. In another example, a tile wainscot wall treatment with a contrasting decorative tile just below the coved finish tile piece would create a horizontal line.

In a kitchen, an oversized 2- to 4-inch thick countertop in a contrasting color introduces a strong horizontal line. For a Traditional space, upper cabinet doors with a double panel design that features a 9- to 14-inch panel at the top of the cabinet will create a horizontal shape along the upper portion of the elevation.

Figure 3.1 *Kitchen Featuring Horizontal Lines*
The contrasting striped molding featured above the wall cabinets creates a horizontal line that is reinforced by the dark molding below the wall cabinets, the contrasting countertop, the dark toe kick at the base of the island and the accent tile on the hood and backsplash. (Courtesy of American Woodmark)

Figure 3.2 *Kitchen Featuring Horizontal Lines*
Horizontal lines are created in this elegant room by mixing small stripes of a darker colored tile within the limestone wall. (Courtesy of Fu-Tung Cheng – Berkeley, California. Photography by Matthew Millman)

Figure 3.3 *Bathroom Featuring Horizontal Lines*
Extending the mirror over the toilet and the open nature of the vanity elongate the space with horizontal lines. (Courtesy of Vernon Applegate and Gioi Ngoc Tran – San Francisco, California)

Vertical Line

A vertical line carries the eye upward and adds visual height to the space. It expresses forcefulness and can have a formal, austere feeling. Some viewers interpret vertical lines as being rigid. Vertical lines can be created by a patterned surface, by contrasting colors of the same material or by combining dissimilar materials along one elevation of the room.

Be aware that the width of the line, the space between the lines, and the contrast between the finish of the line and adjacent spaces all affect the impact of vertical lines. Narrow pinstripe lines feel softer than strong, wide bands of contrasting color. Closely spaced, thin lines can visually widen a room rather than add height.

Figure 3.4 *Kitchen Featuring Vertical Lines*
Vertical lines in the beaded board surround on the peninsula are repeated in the hood. (Courtesy of Dura Supreme)

Figure 3.5 *Bathroom Featuring Vertical Lines*
The contrasting tall cabinet placed at the end of the vanity, chrome storage cylinder and dark material capping the wall between the shower and water closet visually increase the height of the room by concentrating on strong vertical lines. (Courtesy of Tim Scott and Erica Westeroth, CKD – Toronto, Ontario)

Curved Line

The infinite variety of curved lines makes them useful in expressing both contemporary and traditional feelings. A full curve suggests joy. A soft curve suggests refinement. A curve at one angle denotes happiness. Turned upside-down, the same curved line suggests sorrow.

Curved lines have a feminine feeling and generally soften space. They work well in the bathroom environment, which is generally made up of hard-edged and hard-textured surfaces. Think about adding two curved cabinet fronts in a master suite, or curving the counter surface over rectangular vanity units. A kitchen mantel hood area may be accentuated with a curved apron panel. Introducing a curved line in the counter surface can dramatically soften island ends.

Figure 3.6 *Kitchen Featuring Curved Lines*
Arched cabinet bonnet details are repeated above the refrigerator and window. (Courtesy of Daniel Lenner, CMKBD and co-designer Madelane Shane – Allentown, Pennsylvania)

Figure 3.7 *Kitchen Featuring Curved Lines*
Curved molding details, as well as curved cabinet shapes at
the top of the armoire and at the cooking area, combine to
create a welcoming kitchen. (Courtesy of Rutt HandCrafted
Cabinetry)

Diagonal Line

A diagonal line is dramatic. It forces the eye in either a horizontal or vertical direction. It can have a jagged sense about it. A diagonal line implies action and movement. It has an energetic, vibrant feeling that can sometimes be disconcerting or disturbing. Much like vertical lines, diagonal lines that don't contrast strongly with the background are easier to view in a small, confined space than are large, contrasting statements.

For example, a kitchen may feature a dramatic angled line in the stainless hood located above the cooking center. Such a line can contrast with the backsplash material, or repeat it if steel is specified for this area. Another interesting way to use an angled line is to install decorative ceramic or stone tiles on the diagonal along the backsplash or a shower area in the bathroom.

Some kitchens are very small, and most bathrooms are limited in space, so the impact of diagonal lines can be overpowering. Think about the overall impact of the lines you are creating with the arrangement of cabinetry, accessories, surface treatments and walls within the bathroom or small kitchen by visualizing the space, or detailing elevations or a perspective.

Figure 3.8 *Kitchen Featuring Diagonal Lines*
Diagonal lines are featured in the backsplash and on the floor. The change in scale between these two surfaces is a good example of design gradation. (Courtesy of Erica Westeroth, CKD and Tim Scott – Toronto, Canada)

Figure 3.9 *Bathroom Featuring Diagonal Lines*
An artistic window consisting of vibrantly colored diagonal glass panes adds an effective focal point to this small bathroom. (Courtesy of Michelle Drenckhahn – St. Louis, Missouri)

COMBINING LINES

Lines can be used to create a space that is restful or active, peaceful or busy. Too many of any one type of line may be visually uninteresting. On the other hand, too many contrasting lines cause visual confusion and shrink the perception of space, especially in a small room. If you are unsure, it is probably wise to err on the conservative side when arranging lines within a kitchen or bathroom. A simple room can always be enhanced with accessories later. It's difficult to tone down an overdone room.

SHAPE

Line is the simplest element of a shape; each shape is a configuration of lines. Therefore, lines make up shapes, which can be used to change the way the space is perceived.

The simple shapes used in design are rectangular, square, diagonal, triangular and curved.

- **Rectangular Shape**. Because of its horizontal nature, it is an easy shape for many people to relate to.

- **Square Shape**. Can be used within a small space quite comfortably. However, little visual movement is created with a square. Its stagnant nature can lead to an uninteresting room.

- **Diagonal or Angled Shape**. Is the least stable and gives the impression of movement. The shape is very strong and, by virtue of this power, dominates the design. Be aware, an angled shape introduced into a room that has more than four sides begins to take on the characteristics of a circle as the number of sides increases.

- **Triangular Shape**. Is most stable when its base is at the bottom of the elevation or space.

- **Curved or Circular Shape**. Visually stretches a space by allowing the eye to move continuously throughout. A curved shape dominates over a square or a rectangular one because the eye naturally follows around the complete circle, as opposed to focusing on each separate wall of a square or a rectangle.

Figure 3.10 *Kitchen Designed with Rectangular Shapes*
This small New York City kitchen combines a horizontal
soffit molding stripe with a diagonal "quilted" pattern on the
stainless steel refrigerator front. The framed refrigerator
panels, the doorway, a pass-through counter area and glass
fronted cabinets are all boxy, rectangular, tall shapes that
unify the design. (Courtesy of Rochelle Kalisch, CKD –
Brooklyn, New York. Photography by Maura McEvoy)

Figure 3.11 *Home Office Designed with Rectangular Shapes*
An adult retreat, which combines a home office, bar area and entertainment center, is a study of rectangular shapes —seen in both the door paneling and open bookcase sections. (Courtesy of Peter Ross Salerno, CMKBD and co-designer Joyce Dixion – Wyckoff, New Jersey)

Figure 3.12 *Kitchen Designed with Square Shapes*
Glass inserts in a variety of the cabinet doors create a room with a concentration of square shapes. (Courtesy of Gioi Ngoc Tran – San Francisco, California)

Figure 3.13 *Kitchen Designed with Diagonal or Angled Shapes*
In this contemporary kitchen, the hand-cut edge on the stone splash creates a diagonal shape. Note the repetition of this shape in the table leg in the foreground. (Courtesy of Susan Bates – Los Altos, California)

Figure 3.14 *Bathroom Designed with Diagonal or Angled Shapes*
The gothic pointed arch valances combined with a similar shape in the cornice molding create a unique bathroom. (Courtesy of Julie A. Stoner, CKD, ASID – Wayne, Pennsylvania)

Figure 3.15 *Kitchen Designed with Triangular Shapes*
Stepping the metallic tile down each side of the hood area creates a triangular shaped pattern. (Courtesy of Wood-Mode Inc., Designed by Ron Gustafson – Downers Grove, Illinois)

Figure 3.16 *Kitchen Designed with Curved or Circular Shapes*
The rounded island shape is repeated in the curved dish rack. (Courtesy of Dan McFadden and co-designer Debbie Larsen – Geneva, Illinois)

Figure 3.17 *Bathroom Designed with Curved or Circular Shapes*
The vanity cabinetry features a curved apron molding and a curved backsplash shape. (Courtesy of Martha Gargano and co-designer Karen Sciascia – Cheshire, Connecticut)

IDENTIFYING PATTERN PREFERENCE

After becoming familiar with various lines and shapes, designers can combine them into patterns that appeal to the client and support the design theme. Patterns are made up of elements of design: notably line and shape. A "pattern" can be defined as something the eye follows. It is the arrangement of designs. Design patterns are also classified in five broad categories. Designers who can identify the client's preference will quickly find the most appropriate direction to follow in material recommendations.

The five broad categories are:

- Structural

- Naturalistic

- Stylized

- Geometric

- Abstract

All offer possibilities in keeping with both the style and mood of different motifs. Following are a series of kitchens and bathrooms that include these various patterns.

Structural

Structural patterns allow the structure of the product to determine the form of the design. Enrichment and pattern come from the materials used. There is little, if any, applied ornamentation. The grain in woods, cabinetry or floors, the veins in slate, the specks in granite or stone-like surface materials all fall into the category of structural pattern. Clients who prefer natural presentation of materials often choose structural design.

Figure 3.18 *Kitchen with Structural Pattern*
The floor, solid surface work surfaces and plants support the subtle graining of the wood cabinets and texture of the tumbled marble splash and granite raised counter. The structural pattern of the materials themselves presents the only pattern. (Courtesy of Paulette Hessinger, CKD – Erie, Pennsylvania. Photography by Pete Gool)

Figure 3.19 *Bathroom with Structural Pattern*
The texture and pattern of the multi-colored slate, with its
hand-cut edge flowing across the wall behind the glass
lavatory and counter, provide pattern interest in this small
bathroom. (Courtesy of Beverly Staal, CKD, CBD –
Kirkland, Washington. Photography by Roger Turk)

37

Naturalistic

Naturalistic patterns represent subject matter drawn from nature, such as flowers, leaves, fruits, animals and landscapes. The motif is as realistic as possible. The colors are frequently related to those found in nature. Such designs are typically seen in decorative ceramic tiles, custom painted murals, wallpaper patterns or borders and fabrics selected for the kitchen or bathroom space. The patterns lend themselves to either formal or informal transitional rooms.

Figure 3.20 *Kitchen with Naturalistic Pattern*
Naturalistic patterns are often created for ceramic tile murals. (Courtesy of Karen Williams – New York, New York. Photography by Peter Leach)

Figure 3.21 *Bathroom with Naturalistic Pattern*
Powder rooms provide the ideal space for an exuberant design statement. This guest bathroom combines trompe l'oeil limestone walls in ruin with a pastoral scene beyond. (Trompe l'oeil means "to fool the eye." At first glance the viewer senses reality, then discovers it is not real at all.) Such a clear focus on realism is a unique example of naturalistic design. (Courtesy of Peter Ross Salerno, CMKBD – Wyckoff, New Jersey)

Stylized

Stylized patterns are drawn from recognized natural sources, but the pattern makes no pretense at actual representation. The themes used are simplified, exaggerated, rearranged or distorted to achieve the purposes of the design. A stencil pattern on the wall in a Pennsylvania farmhouse kitchen is an example of a stylized pattern. Such patterns are also often selected for wallpaper or border choices. Many ceramic tile decorative patterns feature a stylized motif.

Figure 3.22 *Kitchen with Stylized Pattern*
A ceramic tile border separating the solid surface worktop and the diagonally placed white tile splash is a stylized presentation of a grape vine. (Courtesy of Nancy L. Boriack – Fairfax, Virginia. Photography by Hadley Photography)

Figure 3.23 *Bathroom with Stylized Pattern*
An avant-garde bathroom uses stylized human figures for
cabinet hardware. (Courtesy of Sandra L. Steiner-Houck,
CKD – Mechanicsburg, Pennsylvania)

Geometric

Geometric patterns follow mathematically predictable formulas. Circles, triangles, rectangles, stripes, plaids, polka dots and lacy patterns are all based on geometric forms. This type of pattern works extremely well when colors or shapes of the same naturalistic materials are combined. Transitional and modern kitchens and bathrooms, which typically have little applied ornamentation, often showcase geometric patterns.

Figure 3.24 *Kitchen with Geometric Pattern*
The glass block backsplash and brick shaped tile floor are both examples of geometric patterns. (Courtesy of Ellen Cheever, CMKBD, ASID – Wilmington, Delaware)

Figure 3.25 *Bathroom with Geometric Pattern*
Visual interest in this neutral bathroom is supplied by the geometric tile pattern on the floor and shower walls. The designer has used various sizes of neutral beige and taupe tiles to create the pattern. (Courtesy of Diane Foreman, CKD – Redmond, Washington)

Abstract

Abstract patterns are based on geometric form, but introduce an element of impressionism and artistic freedom. The shapes and patterns are less rigid and formal than the traditional concept of geometric design. Such a pattern may work well along the backsplash, or at a custom hood in kitchens. Bathrooms may feature an abstract pattern within the tub area, shower walls or floor.

Figure 3.26 *Kitchen with Abstract Pattern*
The vibrant color combination in the cabinet finishes creates an abstract pattern in the space. (Courtesy of Pietro Giorgi, Sr., CMKBD and Ellen Cheever, CMKBD, ASID – Wilmington, Delaware. Photography by McClain Imagery)

Figure 3.27 *Bathroom with Abstract Pattern*
The abstract shape of this hand-made vanity is an excellent example of abstract design. Rather than a typical square space, this powder room is a curved shape. The curved/angled base supports the half-round vanity countertop. (Courtesy of Laurie Carroll – Tucson, Arizona)

SPACE AND FORM

SPACE

The overall room, with its doors and windows, ceiling height and millwork is the "envelope" you work within. It is the space people move around in and which objects occupy.

A kitchen or bathroom space is defined by the objects or forms that occupy the area within the room. The relationship of these parts to the total arrangement of the room becomes the "space." To successfully plan kitchens or bathrooms, it is critical to understand the relationship between the individual form of an object and the overall space (or room) it occupies.

FORM

The form of an object is determined by its structure, apparent weight and ornamentation. Therefore, form is not just the physical shape of the object. Rather, it is determined by the overall structure of the shape and the relationship of that shape with others adjacent to it.

Remember: If the form (visual size) of an object is minimized so it blends with the surrounding space, the form (visual size) of the entire room grows in visual importance. That is why an item in a room seems larger if emphasis is placed on it by contrasting it to adjacent or adjoining objects. A room always appears smaller if there are numerous contrasting items in it.

One way designers emphasize specific forms in a room is to contrast the heights of vertical elements throughout the space. There are three ways that this can be accomplished.

Create a Pyramid: With this approach the tallest vertical element is in the center and adjacent elements grow smaller in descending order.

Create an "H" Form: Taller elements are placed at each end of a run of cabinets. This forms a symmetrically balanced "H" shape. Cabinets resting on the countertop, or extending to the ceiling, may accomplish this. Or use both of these approaches combined along one elevation.

Create a Step Ladder: The tallest element appears at one end of the elevation, with all other elements growing progressively smaller.

Figure 3.28 *Create a Pyramid*
The center cabinet over the sink is raised above the adjacent wall units, creating a pyramid shape. The reduced depth of the cabinet keeps its scale balanced with the other sections of the elevation. (Courtesy of Pietro Giorgi, Sr, CMKBD and Ellen Cheever, CMKBD, ASID – Wilmington, Delaware. Photography by McClain Imagery.)

Figure 3.29 *Create an "H" Form*
By dropping the wall cabinets suspended between the two tall elements, an H shape is created. (Courtesy of Judy Adams Hunt – Sarasota, Florida)

Figure 3.30 *Create a Step Ladder*
The L-shaped display creates a "step ladder" or "staircase" form within the design. The lattice-front cabinet steps down to the tambour cabinet. This unit in turn steps down to the oven cabinet. (Courtesy of Michael Smith, CMKBD – Honolulu, Hawaii)

TEXTURE

There are two types of texture. The first is the actual texture, or the tactile quality of a surface: the sensation one feels when touching the surface. Is it smooth, rough, jagged, soft, hard, cold?

Second is the "visual" texture. The visual quality of an object allows the eye "to feel" the surface rather than the fingers.

Just as the other elements of design trigger emotional responses, so do textures.

- Rough, course textures have a rugged, sturdy quality. They imply a naturalistic pattern.

- Fine, smooth textures suggest formality and elegance. They may imply a hard, cold feeling within the room.

Remember: Consider the texture of the various surfaces as you specify them.

- As a general rule, casual environments work best with strongly textured surfaces.

- Soft, gentle textures support delicate, feminine environments.

- Classically traditional rooms usually include smooth surfaces and soft, curved shapes.

- Contemporary modern rooms work well with smooth surfaces and strong textures combined.

Combining various textures or massing one texture throughout the space are two effective ways to have the room's design focus on the nature of the texture. This focus will appeal to clients who appreciate the beauty of natural materials: wood, granite, ceramic and heavy stuccoed wall surfaces.

Figure 3.31 *Kitchen with Rugged Textures*
The oak grain cabinetry is set off by an arched stone cooking niche and wood beams in this kitchen where strong textures dominate. (Courtesy American Woodmark)

Figure 3.32 *Kitchen with Smooth Textures*
Smooth textures are used in this kitchen with gloss finishes
repeated on the cabinets, granite counters and tile floor.
(Courtesy of Karen Edwards, CMKBD – Bedford Hills,
New York. Photography by Peter Margonelli)

Figure 3.33 *Kitchen Combining Textures*
A rustic masonry partition is combined with gloss granite
surfaces and straight grained veneered cabinet doors.
(Courtesy of Timothy Huber, CKD – Phoenix, Arizona)

Figure 3.34 *Contemporary Bathroom Combining Smooth and Rugged Textures*
This elegant bathroom features wall surfaces finished with a heavily textured ceramic tile. Note the staggered floor pattern combined with the square pattern on the wall—an excellent way to plan tile in a bathroom to eliminate the problematic grout lineup where floor meets wall. A subtle horizontal stripe of decorative tile is artistically placed in the shower enclosure. The solid surface shower bench, shower curve and wall caps soften the effect of the tile. (Courtesy of Steven M. Levine, CKD, CBD and Lonne Weinstein – Madison, Connecticut. Photography by Andrew Bordwin)

COLOR

Because color appeals directly to emotions, it is a fascinating and powerful tool to work with. An explanation of the technical details of color follows.

To become a more astute color specialist, increase your color sensitivity by paying particular attention to colors that surround you every day. Look at magazine ads. Study the sets in a television program you are viewing. Pay attention to the colors used in a store window display.

As your comfort level about color matures, your inhibitions about following the rules of combining colors will begin to disappear and you will gain a freer approach to color expressions.

HUE

Colors are visible when light passes through a prism. The technical name given to a color as it is reflected through a prism is "hue."

When a band of visible light is bent into a circle, a color wheel is created. Often, color wheels are shown with yellow at the top. As long as the colors are correctly arranged, there is no absolute top or bottom to the wheel. The true value and intensity of each hue, as seen in nature, is reflected on the color wheel.

The objects in a room exhibit a particular color because of the selective nature by which their surfaces reflect and absorb light. As light strikes the colored surface, certain wave lengths are reflected to a greater extent than others. This reflected color determines what we see. White surfaces reflect all wave lengths equally and absorb little energy. Black surfaces absorb all wave lengths; therefore we see the virtual absence of color.

COLOR CATEGORIES

There are twelve hues on the color wheel divided into three categories. Remember, the primary and secondary colors and the tertiary colors follow naturally.

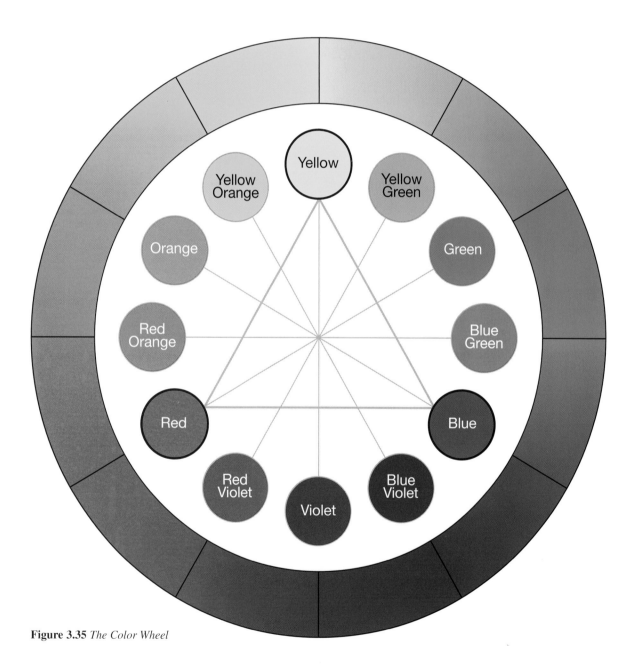

Figure 3.35 *The Color Wheel*

Hue is that attribute of a color by which we distinguish red from green, blue from yellow, etc. There is a natural order of hues: red, yellow, green, blue, violet. One can mix paints of adjacent colors in this series and obtain a continuous variation from one color to the other. For example, red and yellow may be mixed in any proportion to obtain all the hues from red through orange to yellow. The same may be said of yellow and green, green and blue, blue and violet, and violet and red.

Consider a color wheel with twelve equally spaced hues divided as follows:

Primary Hues: Colors from which all others are created. The primary colors are red, yellow and blue. They are equally spaced from one another on the color wheel.

Secondary Hues: Combine two primary hues and the result is a secondary hue. Therefore, they are equally spaced between the primaries. Yellow and blue create green. Blue and red create violet. Red and yellow create orange.

Tertiary Hues: When you combine an adjacent primary and secondary color, tertiary colors are formed. They are always named with the primary color first, followed by the secondary color. Tertiary hues are yellow-green, blue-green, blue-violet, red-violet, red-orange, and yellow-orange.

Color Value

The lightness or darkness of a color is the second way we can affect it. White is the highest value and black the lowest. Mixing white with the hue, called a "tint," produces a high value of a color. Pink is a tint of red. When mixing black with the hue produces a low value of a color, it is called a "shade." A deep Colonial Red is a shade of red.

Figure 3.38 *Value Scale*

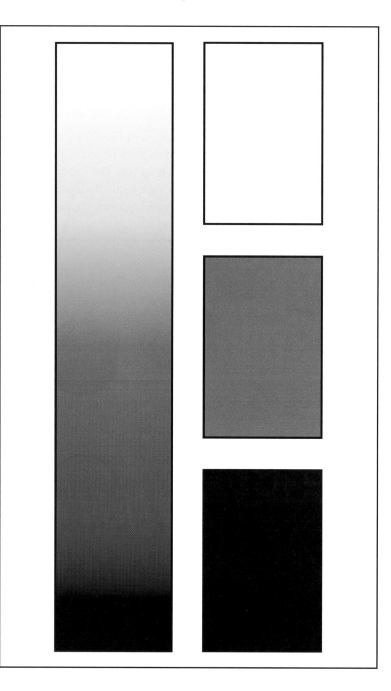

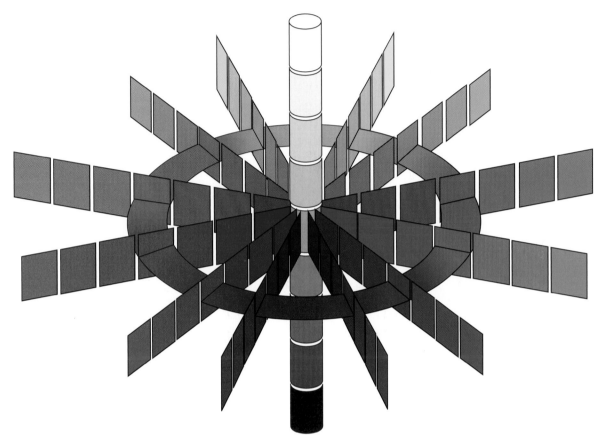

Figure 3.39 *Three-dimensional Color Wheel Reflecting Each Hue's Chroma and Value*

COLOR HARMONY

Specific color harmonies are created in the following arrangements:

Analogous

Analogous with Complementary Accent

Triad

Figure 3.40 *Graphically Understanding Color Harmonies*

Complementary

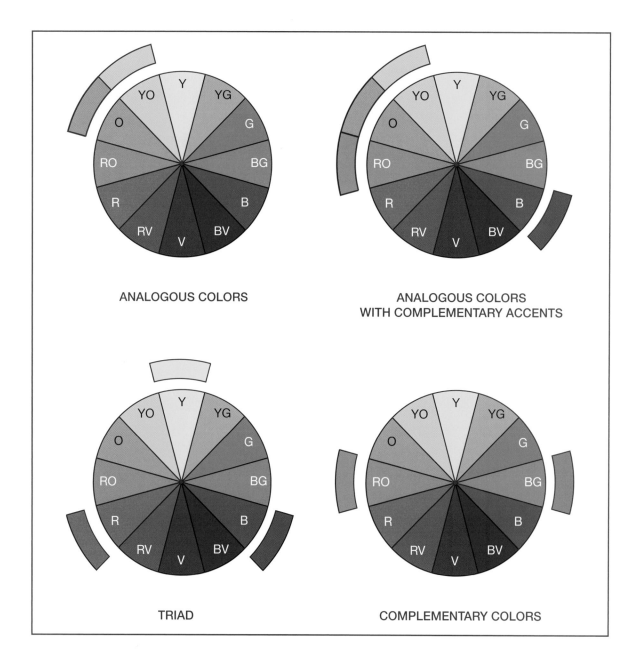

ANALOGOUS COLORS

ANALOGOUS COLORS
WITH COMPLEMENTARY ACCENTS

TRIAD

COMPLEMENTARY COLORS

Monochromatic

A harmony in which many shades, tints or tones of a single color are used. For example, a bisque countertop and fixtures, tan floor, brown cabinets and a combination of the three colors used in the wall covering. The beige tint and brown tone create a scheme developed from the principal orange hue. In order to relieve monotony, the scheme may use black, white or an intense pure color in addition to a variety of textures.

Figure 3.41 *Kitchen with Monochromatic Color Scheme*
The golden tones of counters, cabinets and wall finish are all drawn from the yellow/orange family. (Courtesy of Rick Farrell – Pickering, Canada)

Figure 3.42 *Bathroom with Mono-chromatic Color Scheme*
In this bathroom, various subtle tones, tints and shades drawn from the yellow family are featured in the marble, cabinet finish, carpet and paint color. (Courtesy of Charles S. Cook – Glencoe, Illinois)

Analogous

A harmony in which colors adjacent to one another on the color wheel are used. One color dominates. The colors may vary in value and intensity. Depending on the colors, the overall scheme is warm or cool. For example, maple cabinets and stainless steel appliances combined with sage green laminate, solid surface or stone counters, with the room finished with a slate green floor. Yellow, yellow-green and green are adjacent to one another on the color wheel.

Figure 3.43 *Bath with Analogous Color Scheme*
In this bath, yellow and yellow greens are combined in the wall color, wood tones and tile. (Courtesy of Jacuzzi)

Analogous with a Complementary Accent

A harmony that accents the analogous color relationship with a color that is opposite on the color wheel. For example, the addition of violet or red accents in a decorative stone backsplash accent added into the analogous scheme described on page 65. Yellow is opposite violet and green is opposite red on the color wheel, and establishes the complementary accent.

Figure 3.44 *Kitchen with Analogous and Complementary Accent Color Scheme*
The violets and pinks in the seating fabric accent the vibrant yellows and greens adjacent to one another on the color wheel. (Courtesy of Linda McLain, CKD – Charleston, South Carolina)

Triad

A harmony in which three colors are used that are equidistant from one another on the color wheel. For example, the three primaries (yellow, blue and red) may be used with intense colors to create a happy, light theme. Or, the yellow may be toned to gold, the red shaded to claret and the blue to indigo to create an elegant, luxurious theme.

Figure 3.45 *Triad Color Scheme*
Red, blue-green and yellow are combined in this room. The pale creamy tint of the floor and the bolder brass fixtures are drawn from the yellow family. Reds are introduced in the accent paint color and taupe wainscot panel finish. A blue-green stone counter finishes the color scheme. (Courtesy of Kaye Hathaway, CKD, ASID – Barrington, Illinois)

Complementary

A harmony that features colors opposite one another on the color wheel. One color is always warm and the other is always cool. To successfully use a complementary scheme, maintain the natural value of the colors. For example, bone and navy blue. The naturally lighter orange (bone) is directly opposite the naturally darker blue.

Figure 3.46 *Complementary Color Scheme*
The island's deep blue granite countertop and cabinetry contrast with the dramatic copper hood and terra cotta toned tile. (Courtesy of Tom Trzcinski, CMKBD – Pittsburgh, Pennsylvania. Photography by Craig Thompson Photography)

Figure 3.47 *Complementary Color Scheme*
Purple and gold were used by the designer to create the look and feel of Egypt. (Courtesy of Tess Giuliani, CKD – Ridgewood, New Jersey)

Neutral

A harmony in which black, white and gray are used. An accent of a brilliant color is sometimes needed to create an interesting combination.

Figure 3.48 *Neutral Color Scheme*
In this kitchen, gray and white cabinets and counters create a monochromatic color scheme. Interest is added by the interplay of textures and shapes and the checkerboard backsplash tile detail. (Courtesy of Wood-Mode Inc.)

Figure 3.49 *Neutral Color Scheme*
This dramatic bath focuses on a neutral blue-gray/white/black
color scheme featured in the tile, fixtures and wall finishes.
(Courtesy of Peter Ross Salerno, CMKBD and co-designer
Tracy Ann Salerno – Wyckoff, New Jersey)

COLOR AND ITS EMOTIONAL IMPACT

Colors have an emotional impact on the viewer. A review of how color affects people follows.

Yellow

According to Rebecca Ewing, a color specialist, "Yellow increases irritability: therefore more arguments occur in a yellow kitchen! Yellow also stimulates the appetite and enhances memory retention (think of a yellow legal pad, yellow highlighter, or yellow Post-it Note)."

Yellow will always remain an important part of the kitchen palette because it is sunny, bright and a happy color that works well with the natural color of food products. Whether a buttery golden tone reflecting the creamy sense of meringues, or a punchy, vibrant look reminiscent of a bouquet of daffodils, yellow can wash across the cabinets or be used as an accent. Yellow has become more intriguing recently as it entered the world of metallic golden tones.

Green

A comment from Rebecca Ewing: "The eyes see green as a neutral, the body treats it as a neutral. It's a suburban color indicating moderation, temperate behavior. In that it is the color of the earth, it provides true balance."

Green can be used as a dark, yellow-green that has been inspired by nature and its serenity, as well as a mauve silver-green that works well with neutrals and complementary colors. In the past, green was sometimes avoided, seen as a uniform or work clothing color. Today, it's a fresh, embraceable hue. It is often used as a neutral backdrop behind a stronger accent color.

Blue

A comment from Rebecca Ewing: "Blue reminds us of water. It slows the body system down; we feel we have all the time in the world. It is the color of logic, leading one to think conceptually. And good news, dieters: it depresses the appetite."

Blue—awash with white—continues to be a strong color preference and is popular in both kitchens and bathrooms. Navy or dark, rich blues are often specified for long-term living environments. Blue is an excellent complementary color to the orange hues seen in ginger, cinnamon or honey tones in other surfaces. Lighter, washed denim blue is another variation on the use of this color.

Purple

A comment from Rebecca Ewing: "Purple is a regal color often times associated with the spiritual, with wealth and with stature."

Home fashion leaders, the European press and some women clothiers continually predict that purple will be an emerging color in the future—but for most consumers, it's just too hard to live with on a permanent basis. It may be just right for an infrequently used, yet dramatic guest powder room.

Reds and Pinks

A comment from Rebecca Ewing: "It's the longest color wave. It sells food because people eat more and pay more in a red environment. Red lets us feel that we can focus on the impulse, indulge ourselves, have the courage or knowledge to be truly individualistic, and live for the present moment." Interestingly enough, pink—a version of red—has a much different impact from its strong red foundation color. "A natural stress reducer, it stimulates our interest in sweet, sugary things," says Ewing.

Red is used extensively in the fashion world to anchor black. It is an excellent accent color, and is seen in dark, vibrant, merlot-type finishes on woods, and in some solid surfacing and quartz countertop materials.

Oranges and Browns

A comment from Rebecca Ewing: "Orange in the past didn't have much 'snob appeal.' However, orange is playful, fun and pleasurable."

Global color trends are leading designers to see a new use of intense orange tones in heavily structured geometric patterns emerging from the African and South American communities. This interest in orange is moving the color into a deeper, richer tone.

Browns—in many cases simply a tone of orange—are safe colors, oftentimes specified by the ultra-conservative. However, they are being given a new life as they become textural mixed with metallics. The dark, earthy brown colors of oak and cherry are used in the furniture world. These brown tones are returning to popularity in kitchen and bathroom settings.

TRANSFORMING SPACE WITH COLOR

You can alter the visual feeling of a space with color. Use the following techniques to change the way a space feels.

- Through the advancing properties of the color, use warm colors and shades to make the room seem smaller or to make an object in the room seem bigger.

- Through the receding properties of the color, use cool colors to make the room seem bigger or to make an object appear smaller.

- Use light colors to decrease the weight of an object and therefore increase the overall spatial perception of the area.

- Use dark colors to increase the weight of an object and to decrease the spatial perception of the total area.

- Use the same color throughout an area to camouflage structural problems.

- Use heavily textured surfaces to absorb light and dull the intensity of a color if you wish to decrease the apparent size and add warmth to the item.

- Use smooth, shiny surfaces to reflect light and to intensify the color of an object, which will increase its apparent size.

If you wish to create a spatial illusion by using color, try these color techniques.

- To expand space via color:

  Use cool colors.

  Use light colors.

  Use dull colors.

  Keep contrasts to a minimum.

- To shrink space with color:

  Use warm colors.

  Use dark colors.

  Use bright colors.

  Introduce several contrasts.

- To lower a ceiling with color:

    Use warm colors.

    Use dark tones.

    Use strong saturation.

- To heighten a ceiling with color:

    Use cool colors.

    Use light tints.

- To shorten a room with color, on the narrow wall of the room:

    Use warm colors.

    Use dark colors.

    Use a strong saturation.

- To lengthen a room with color:

    Use cool colors.

    Use light colors.

    Use dull colors.

    Limit contrasts.

A CLOSING COMMENT ON THE IMPORTANCE OF COLOR

For years, the design wisdom has been to use simple, quiet colors on major surfaces, saving punchy tones, tints and shades as accents. However, there seems to be a counterpoint to this safe use of neutrals and gentler colors.

Global economic power shifts, plus world-wide communications have led to a shift in design leadership from the Western European community, which has always looked toward soft neutral color palettes in hard goods and home furnishings. Although we are still strongly influenced by Western European styling, today there are new influences from Africa, from the Mediterranean countries and from South American designers resulting in more vibrant interiors.

The importance of color? A recent Yankelovich survey indicated 39% of consumers are likely to change brands of a product if they can't get the color they want. That's proof of the power of color.

CHAPTER 4: The Principles of Design

The individual tools of design must be organized and arranged. The principles of design: **balance**, **rhythm** and **emphasis** provide a "rule book" or guidelines for how to combine the elements of design.

BALANCE

Presenting a vista to the viewer that offers different areas of equal interest to the eye is what balance is all about. This means bringing equilibrium or stability to the space. Balance is employed to the left and right of a center point, and at the top and bottom of an elevation or wall area. Studies have found that people react most favorably to the visually heavier weighted object at the lower section of the room. This is one reason why, oftentimes, darker colors or more patterned materials seen at the floor line are more satisfactory than heavily vibrantly colored ceiling surfaces. There are three types of balance to employ when planning a kitchen or bathroom.

- Symmetrical or Formal Balance

- Asymmetrical or Informal Balance

- Radial Balance

Symmetrical Balance

Symmetrical balance occurs when two objects or elements of the room are exactly the same, often identified as a "mirror image" of one another. Balance is obtained by identical forces exerting equal thrust because of their placement and similar distance from the pivot or center of balance. For example, in a kitchen, equal-sized cabinet doors on each side of the sink or each side of a decorative hood create a symmetrically balanced elevation.

In bathroom planning, installing tall cabinets to flank each side of a lavatory area will create symmetrical balance, or locating a mirror centered on a lavatory with wall-mounted sconces on each side will provide the same type of balance.

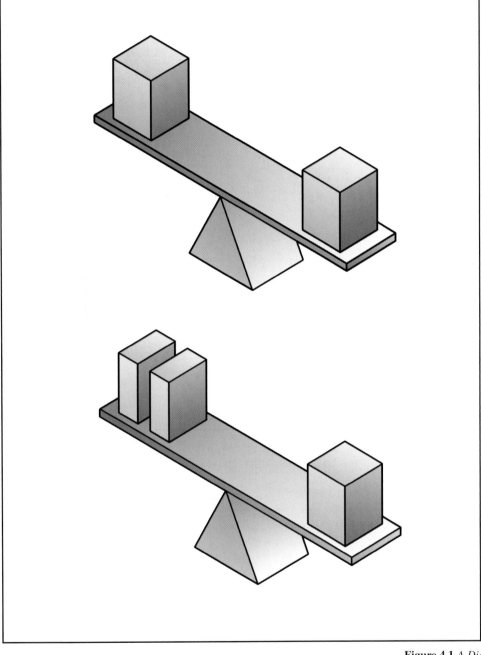

Figure 4.1 *A Diagram of Symmetrical (top) and Asymmetrical Balance (bottom)*

Figure 4.2 *Kitchen Designed with Symmetrical Balance*
The two tall refrigeration units are separated by an open storage area. The two appliances are mirror images of one another, creating a symmetrically balanced elevation. (Courtesy of Frederick A. Flock, CKD, CBD – Sylvan Lake, Michigan)

Figure 4.3 *Bathroom Designed with Symmetrical Balance*
This small powder room features a gentle curve on the small single-door sink cabinet and two identical three-drawer banks on each side. The arrangement is repeated above in the light fixtures flanking the mirror, demonstrating formal symmetrical balance. (Courtesy of Diane Foreman, CKD – Redmond, Washington. Photography by Roger Turk)

Asymmetrical Balance

When unequal forces attract equal attention because of their placement, the resulting equilibrium is called asymmetrical balance. For example, in a kitchen, a wall cabinet that extends down to the counter at the end of a run (its shape is tall and narrow) with glass doors can be asymmetrically balanced by a long horizontal run of enclosed cabinets on the opposite side of the sink. In a bathroom setting, a tiled tub surround at one end of a small bathroom wall can be balanced by an elongated double-bowl vanity and oversized mirror with a decorative light on the opposite side of the room, or as a continuation to the elevation.

Figure 4.4 *Kitchen Designed with Asymmetrical Balance*
Color is used to differentiate, yet unite this asymmetrically balanced kitchen. The "step ladder" cabinetry arrangement over the sink is symmetrically balanced. To the right, the blue cabinet reverses—but echoes—that same shape, symmetrically balancing the blue cabinet. Placing these two differently finished cabinet elevations on opposite walls asymmetrical balances the shapes because the colors are different but equally appealing to the eye. (Courtesy of Gerard Ciccarello, CMKBD – Westbrook, Connecticut)

Figure 4.5 *Kitchen Designed with Asymmetrical Balance*
The corner angled sink is balanced left and right by two very
different cabinets. On the left, a wider, shorter dark cherry
unit with microwave matches the casework in the balance of
the room. To the right, a narrower—yet taller—open accent
piece offers an asymmetrical balance elevation. (Courtesy of
Wood-Mode Inc., Photography by Peter Vitale)

Figure 4.6 *Bathroom Designed with Asymmetrical Balance*
A master suite offers an excellent example of asymmetrical
design by the balance seen between the curved circular
shower to the left of the soaking tub, which finishes at
approximately 84" off the floor, seen against the darker
rectangular wall grid that finishes against a strong vertical
wall element repeating the tile seen elsewhere. The lower
height of the shower and the softer curved shape are balanced
by the dissimilar larger—and darker but straightforward—
back wall featuring both the repetitive grid pattern and the
tile slab at the end of the tub. (Courtesy of Kohler Company,
Designed by Laura Bohn – New York, New York)

Radial

A third type of balance is created when equal forces attract equal attention as they radiate from a central axis. Radial balance is rarely used in kitchen or bathroom design: it is found in table arrangement design and landscape architecture quite frequently.

If you have an opportunity to employ such balance, place one element of the room in the center—a tub enclosure, for example, in a master suite, or an oversized island in a kitchen—and then place all the other elements of the room radiating out from that central point.

Figure 4.7 *Kitchen Designed with Radial Balance*
A round kitchen shape is used at the island and back wall, creating radial balance. (Courtesy of Susan Reese – Indianapolis, Indiana)

CONTINUITY/RHYTHM

How often do you see a room and intuitively feel it "works?" Or look at a space—and although the individual elements may be attractive—you know the overall room doesn't "work." If it does "work," it is because the individual elements in the room have been arranged in a rhythmic way. If not, it is probably a collection of well-designed, but dissimilar elements having no continuity in the way they relate to one another.

The continuity or rhythm within a design is the "glue" that holds the dissimilar elements together. It is what helps to create the unified, total design.

Continuity or rhythm is a matter of forms and lines that divide the space into understandable intervals. Rhythm is obtained in four major ways: repetition, alternation, progression and domination.

Repetitive

Repetition is created when one or more design elements (line, shape, form) are repeated. The viewer's eye will follow the repeated element.

For example, the repetition of a square 6" x 6" tile on a bathroom floor, wainscoting and shower enclosure provides rhythm through repetition; the geometric pattern created by the grout lines and tile shapes keeps the design interesting.

Figure 4.8 *Diagram of Repetitive Rhythm*

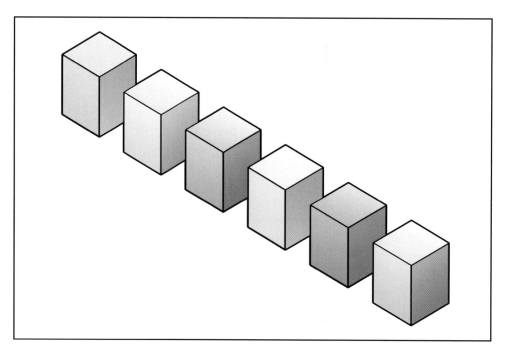

Figure 4.9 *Rhythm Created by Repetitious Design*
The taupe tones in the 12" x 12" tile floor are repeated in
the stone countertop, with two alternating sized patterns of
wallcovering on the walls and soffit. This is a good example
of repetitive rhythm based on the ground color of the floor,
the stone color, and the ground color of the wallpaper.
(Courtesy of Susan Seals – Morristown, Tennessee.
Photography by Jerry Hendricks)

Figure 4.10 *Rhythm Created by Repetitious Design*
The white color in the cabinets is repeated on the stone floor.
The floor has a dark diamond tile insert repeating the
dark marble finish on the vanity countertop. The bathroom
repeats the neutral dark and light scheme throughout the
space, an example of repetitive rhythm. (Courtesy of
Diana Valentine and Diana Wogulis Keys, – Redmond,
Washington. Photography by David Livingston)

Alternation

The selected motif pulls and holds the design together by providing a logical step from one element to the next. The principle of alternation is oftentimes used in decorative tile backsplash designs in kitchens. Or surfacing material used throughout a space with a decorative "alternate" creates a rhythmic design. It may be a stripe, a smaller ceramic element, or simply a change in color.

For example, in kitchen design, a parquet hardwood floor or vinyl patterned floor may provide an alternating rhythm through the space. A change in color from edge, to deck, to splash in solid surface countertop finishes is another example.

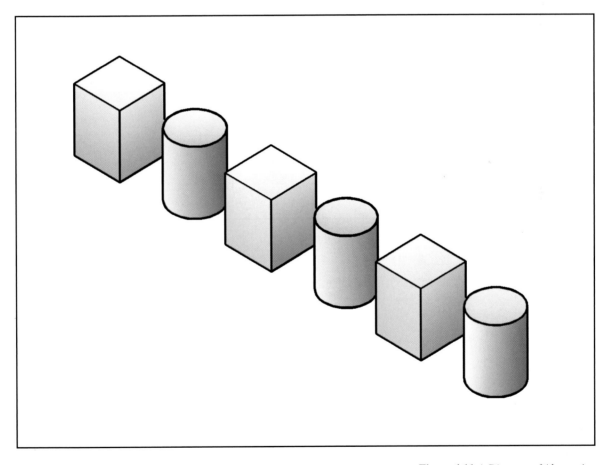

Figure 4.11 *A Diagram of Alternating Rhythm*

Figure 4.12 *Rhythm Created by Alternating Design*
The tile splash along the right hand elevation alternates decorative tile set in two different borders elsewhere in the space. (Courtesy of Pietro Giorgi, Sr., CMKBD and Ellen Cheever, CMKBD, ASID – Wilmington, Delaware. Photography by McClain Imagery)

Figure 4.13 *Rhythm Created by Alternating Design*
Separating two mirrors along the floating vanity is an example of alternating rhythm. The striped effect of the veneer wood grain has an alternating aspect, as well. The floor pattern suggests a progressive rhythm. (Courtesy of Gioi Ngoc Tran and co-designer Vernon Applegate – San Francisco, California)

Progression

- The motif progresses through a series of intermediate steps that carry the eye from one end of the scale to the other. The shape or motif changes in small increments. Gradations (or a progressional change) of colors from dominant shades to more subdued hints are effective.

Changes in square or rectangular floor elements to a smaller size at the deck or backsplash are another example of progressive rhythm.

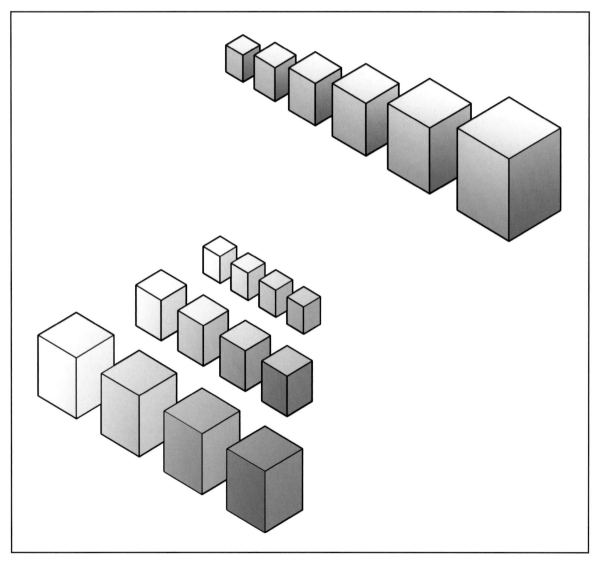

Figure 4.14 *A Diagram of Progressive Rhythm*

Figure 4.15 *Rhythm Created by Progressive Design*
The 4" x 4" square shape of this tumbled stone backsplash tile is seen in a smaller scale on the hood front apron detail. Therefore, the square shape progressively changes in size, creating a rhythmic movement throughout the space. (Courtesy of Sheila Tilander, CKD, CBD – Redmond, Washington)

Figure 4.16 *Rhythm Created by Progressive Design*
The large alternating tile floor pattern features a 1" x 1" mosaic border. The same type and finish of tile is used in 4-1/4" tile on the countertop, with the edging echoing the 1" x 1" size again. (Courtesy of Wendy Yang – Glencoe, Illinois. Photography by Kaskel Architectural Photography, Inc.)

Domination

A predominance of one element causes the eye to follow the lines and shapes created by that element and thus to move in the same direction. Oversized countertop thicknesses, moldings, borders and chair rails that provide a dominant line throughout the space are another examples.

The third principle of design involves the overall center of interest. The focal point in the design is carefully crafted so the eye of the viewer is drawn to it.

To create a focal point within a space, include three levels of "attention-grabbing" design: dominant, sub-dominant and subordinate. A dominant theme captures the sense of the space. A second layer of sub-dominant elements is not as important as your key element—but they accent that key element. Lastly, subordinate elements add definition to the total design.

Area Emphasis

Emphasizing one area is particularly appropriate in creating a focal point in both kitchens and bathrooms. You may wish to highlight the hood or window area in a kitchen, or the vanity area in a bathroom. In many designs today, a kitchen sink cabinet literally protrudes beyond the adjacent cabinetry, with an elegant valance framing the window above. This creates a total center of interest as one enters the space. The same treatment is oftentimes used in hood areas. The vanity in a bathroom or a luxurious spa tub arrangement framed by windows are ideal spots to create area emphasis.

EMPHASIS: THE FOCAL POINT

Figure 4.17 *Area Emphasis*
The extended custom hood used along the back wall of this Old World kitchen creates an impressive focal point. (Courtesy of Showcase/V6B Design Group, Vancouver, British Columbia)

Figure 4.18 *Area Emphasis*
The same room features an oversized island, which repeats the proportions of the hood wall. (Courtesy of Showcase/ V6B Design Group, Vancouver, British Columbia)

Figure 4.19 *Area Emphasis*
With its dramatic use of vivid tile, the back wall becomes the focal point of this kitchen. The harlequin pattern not only run across the backsplash but also swoops up to the ceiling behind the hood. (Courtesy of KraftMaid Cabinetry)

Figure 4.20 *Area Emphasis*
Arched elements above the sink and the cooking surface in this monochromatic kitchen demonstrate how an overall room can quietly provide emphasis. (Courtesy of Mark White, CKD – Annapolis, Maryland. Photography by Kaskel Architectural Photography, Inc.)

Theme Emphasis

You can also create emphasis by allowing the surface selection and the style of the space to dominate the room. This is often seen in heavily detailed rooms where the dominant pattern of material or woodworking details creates a cohesive environment.

Figure 4.21 *Theme Emphasis*
The naturalistic theme is introduced in the pebble floor and wood frame accents. Note the interesting shapes created by varying the counter heights. (Courtesy of Tess Giuliani, CKD – Ridgewood, New Jersey)

Figure 4.22 *Theme Emphasis*
The emphasis on the sweeping view of nature seen through the windows is supported by the textured materials and repeated use of wood in this bathroom. (Courtesy of Beverly Staal, CKD, CBD – Kirkland, Washington.)

CONCLUSION

It is important to note that good design is never an accident and—no matter how small the kitchen or bathroom—design is a major part of the planning process. The space must be pleasing to the eye, as well as functionally planned. It should be created so it "stands the test of time."

A good way to understand this sense of "timeless design" is to consider the difference between style and fashion. Being in-fashion means being willing to listen to others dictate what is beautiful. Style is much more lasting. It is about being free because of the solution's appropriateness for the environment. Whereas fashion encloses or defines, style invites. Whereas fashion demands acceptance, style is individualized. Fashion so often seems just a moment too new or, at worst, just a moment too old while style moves with ease and timeless grace.

Fashion is not to be ignored. It is a designer's tool, but it is not a dictate. Employing the elements and principles of design will assist you in building a stylish environment that will be well-suited to the client, which will "stand the test of time" and still be considered beautiful years after the project is completed.

CHAPTER 5: Creating a Theme Environment

After you have a clear understanding of the elements and principles of design, your next step in learning how to adapt generic design training to your specific kitchen and bathroom planning is to understand how to create rooms that follow historical themes or include key elements of current modern interiors.

A client may show you a picture that is reminiscent of a cottage in the English countryside or a sleek apartment in New York. They may use words such as "Old World," "Pacific Rim," and "Scandinavian Cottage." You need not be an expert in each of these design themes, but you must have a working knowledge of the history behind these styles and a clear understanding of the attributes of such spaces, which are transferable to rooms created in the 21st Century.

ESTABLISHING A THEME FOR A KITCHEN OR BATHROOM PROJECT

Establishing a theme for the kitchen or bathroom helps you organize the project. Once a definite style is identified, many possibilities are automatically eliminated and a more manageable range of choices can be presented to the client. This saves you time during the planning process.

Designers often wonder, "How do I know what is appropriate for a specific architectural style?" The question is difficult to answer because there are few guidelines to follow. Many architectural periods have distinctive furniture styles, but they had no kitchens or bathrooms for us to study. Therefore, we must adapt furniture to cabinetry and draperies to shower curtains. We must also contend with the functional requirements of modern appliances and bath fixtures and fittings.

Our most practical recommendation—to successfully create a room reminiscent of the past, strive for the feeling of the requested style rather than an actual reproduction of products of the period.

To accomplish this you must first understand architecture; second, you must be familiar with the furniture, styles and fashions of each era; and, third, you must be able to translate this information into an acceptable modern kitchen or bathroom with the appropriate period motif.

THEME STYLING TERMINOLOGY

As you begin to study the history of architecture and understand the homes of our country, specific periods of design and styles of furniture will be identified. These eras are commonly called period styles. To clarify terminology used in this section:

- **Contemporary (or Modern):** A look that reflects the lifestyle of current society. Today, the design combines styles from diverse periods.

- **Country (Rustic):** Rural as distinguished from urban. Used most often to define an informal style.

- **Eclectic:** Composed of elements drawn from various doctrines, methods and styles. Mixing elements of different styles and/or periods.

- **Mid-Century Modern:** A term identifying the post-war 1950 to 1960s design era, which focused on using new building materials, shapes and colors within modern environments. An experimental time in the architectural and industrial design world.

- **Motif:** A reoccurring, salient, thematic element. A motif may be a pattern, design, emblem or object that has become automatically associated with a particular style.

- **Old (Olde) World:** In North America, used by designers to describe design details from European countries, notably the English, Italian and French country homes of the 17th and 18th centuries.

- **Period:** Defines a particular time cycle or series of events in architectural history. Era is another word that means the same thing.

- **Style:** A distinctive quality, form or type of architecture.

- **Traditional:** Refers to designs from past generations that have an established style. In North America, the term is often used to describe architecture and furnishings from the 17th, 18th and 19th centuries.

- **Transitional:** New term used to convey a popular styling of today, which is a combination or midway point between Traditional/Old World and Modern/Contemporary styling. Transitional signifies a passage or evolution from one style to another.

- **Vernacular:** Local adaptation of a formal style, exhibiting notable ethnic and regional interpretations—usually in rural or provincial areas.

ECLECTIC DESIGN

Many of today's consumers are interested in an eclectic, personalized environment suited to their lifestyle. You will often see a Contemporary kitchen with a Corinthian column or an Art Deco chair. Very often Contemporary rooms are greatly enhanced by the addition of a treasured family armoire or sideboard inherited from generations before.

However, there are rules to learn about eclectic design. For example, in rooms where a client wants to "mix and match," the basic style must first be identified: will the client enjoy a Contemporary environment, or one with a more Traditional flair? More about the details of these spaces later.

Following are four broad categories of Eclectic design.

ENHANCING A NEW KITCHEN OR BATHROOM WITH OLD OBJECTS

This is the most typical way eclecticism is applied within a kitchen or bathroom space. A unique vitality is added to the space that embraces the present, the past and the future in one sweeping view. For example, a Contemporary environment favoring visual restraint is more interesting with the addition of a reference to yesterday as its focal point: a single piece of antique furniture with figured wood. This unexpected contrast between new and old accentuates the difference, allowing those enjoying the space to celebrate both what was and what is.

PLACING A NEW KITCHEN OR BATHROOM WITHIN AN OLD SETTING

Eclectic enthusiasts realize the architecture of the home is not compromised if the interior transitions into a more modern room. City loft living spaces are a great example of this. A modern Italian kitchen design may be seen against old brick walls and a well-worn wide plank wood floor.

THE COLLECTOR'S MIX

A collector's kitchen or bathroom interior falls into three broad categories:

- **An overall aesthetic of abundance:** An approach summed up as "planned clutter," with numerous groupings on nearly every space and surface.

- **An artistic presentation:** In contrast, other collectors prefer interiors with a gallery-like quality: providing edited backgrounds that allow one or more collections to be undisputedly in the forefront.

- **A cross-cultural mix:** Some eclectic environments today combine elements from different cultures—the room expresses the owner's personal journey through time and to new places. Cross-cultural eclecticism may be based around an important architectural element found in one's travels: a massive stone table, for example, from the Tuscan region, or artwork from a trip showcased in an otherwise stylized room.

THE SIGNATURE ELEMENT

Some interiors, like individuals, have a particular identifying characteristic that sets them apart. A signature element may take center stage in the space—with the designer using the elements of design (line and form, texture and pattern, color and light, scale and proportion) to allow that signature item to be boldly and clearly the focal point within the overall room.

ARCHITECTURAL HISTORY REVIEW

A BRIEF LOOK AT THE PAST

As kitchen and bathroom planners leaf through magazines and see interiors that are highly stylized, they should realize that Western architecture, throughout its history, has been identified with the character of Western civilization.

Classical architecture from Europe is oftentimes divided into the Classic period (500 BC – 11th Century, The Age of Reason), the Gothic period (12th Century – 16th Century, The Age of Faith), and the Renaissance period (15th Century – 17th Century, The Age of Humanism). It is this Renaissance period many of our architecturally rustic European country settings speak of.

- **Classicism (500 BC – 11th Century):** The design vocabulary that has shaped Western architecture ever since Ancient Greece is characterized by a set of compositional rules and architectural elements, in particular columns and order. It is a language that has continually reinvented itself, providing successive generations the tools to explore the fundamentals of design. Historically, Classicism ruled the architectural world from 500 BC to the 11th Century. It then served as a foundation for guidelines during the Renaissance period (considered to be the "return to Classicism"), as well as for Classical 18th and 19th century architecture and building designs.

- **Gothic (12th Century – 16th Century):** In structural terms, the creation of Gothic architecture marked a major departure from what had gone before. It was based on a sophisticated understanding of the way in which a minimum of structure could carry a maximum of load. Visually, the pointed arch characterized it. Because of the limited patronage of the arts directed by religious leaders, Gothic architecture was also a physical expression of spiritual values and so is suffused with Christian symbolism.

- **Renaissance (15th Century – 17th Century):** The 15th Century rediscovery of Classicism associated with the cultural sophistication of Florence and architecturally associated with the use of the Classic orders.

In North America, the early Puritans arriving in New England, as well as the gentlemen farmers in Jamestown, Virginia, brought treasured family objects and a sense of style from their European homes. Although houses were initially quite rugged, the furnishings within typically demonstrated the style of the owners. As life became easier and monies more available, more formal American styles became common, characterized by ornamentation insignias. This period lasted from approximately 1640 through 1850.

Around the beginning of the 19th century, architecture in the Western world underwent an abrupt change in its nature, as well as in its style because of the effect of the Industrial Revolution. Workers and their families moved from the rural countryside to cities. Homes changed and, therefore, lives changed. New materials became available through the Industrial Revolution, and new demands were placed on buildings.

These changes were not considered good by all—and several artisan and religious movements clearly fought against the styles and lifestyle of Victorian America and the resulting differentiation between the working class and the well-to-do business owners. The Arts & Crafts movement, which began in Europe, quickly moved across the ocean and was a foundation of the design work reflected in Gustav Stickley's Arts & Crafts furniture, the brothers Green and Green and architects creating homes in the Western United States—the foundation of the work of Frank Lloyd Wright.

In addition to changes the Industrial Revolution brought about in the United States, stylistic changes occurred at a rapid pace in Europe, with Napoleon introducing Empire furniture, leading with a more common-man's version oftentimes typified as "Biedermeier Styling" in Austria and Germany. In Paris, the industrial capabilities of new-found technological inventions still led to a yearning for things natural, which led to the Art Nouveau movement.

At the beginning of the 20th Century, a theme for interior design known as "Art Deco" was introduced, and expanded from furniture to architecture after the discovery of King Tut's tomb in the 1920s led to an Egyptian motif focus within the design world. This style gained momentum throughout the beginning of the 20th century, when architects and designers yearned to further strip away the ornamentation of the Victorian era, and maximize the power of industrial invention.

The birth of the International School of Architecture is oftentimes identified as the construction of the Eiffel Tower, commissioned in 1887 to commemorate the exhibition of 1889. The Bauhaus School of Design in Germany, operating until 1930, created the first steel and glass structures. With the advent of World War II, many of these founding European architects moved to the United States, and the International School of Architecture created by these masters dominated through the 1970s.

During the 1950s, 1960s and 1970s, changes were afoot. Individuals found working in these glass, concrete and steel structures in some ways to be dehumanizing. In the 1950s, industrial designers created interesting furniture, experimented with bright, bold colors and fashion accessories. These made both the home and the workspace more visually interesting, creating what we now know of as "Mid-Century Modernism" or "Retro."

In Mexico and the Western region of the United States, designers looked for warmer, more inviting interiors that used materials of the area. The late Michael Taylor, a noted San Francisco interior designer, created the "California look": white wicker, over-scaled furniture, slate floors, tree trunk tables and bleached leather fabrics. Luis Barragan stretched modernism to fit the vernacular of the Mexican garden and added ebullient color with South-of-the-Border bravado in his respected Mexico-based architectural practice, which gave us a foundation for "Southwestern" design.

The architectural community began experimenting with ornamentation in the late 1970s. Michael Graves, an architect known today predominantly for his industrial design work in ergonomically correct, yet architecturally elegant housewares, was recognized as one of the founders of "Post-Modernism" design, which called upon many of the geometric shapes of the Art Deco period, as well as return to the vibrant use of color. The basis of Post-Modernistic design, which influences the emerging Eclectic Transitional spaces of today, is its focus on complexity, not stark simplification. The style synthesizes history and symbolic content rather than relying on purely functional reductionism.

In the 1980s and 1990s, many interior designers returned to the safety, elegance and warmth of European environments: homebuilders created Tuscan villas; kitchens were designed to reflect the inside of these villas, as well. Old World artisan techniques were recreated on everything from wallpaper to tiles with faux painting becoming a highly valued skill.

Throughout the 1990s and into the new century, an emerging interest in softer Contemporary styling based on the sensitivities and sensibilities of the Asian concept of beauty and the calming effects of Pacific Rim design began to emerge. Therefore, many design trend watchers predict we are entering a "Transitional" design period, where more tailored Traditional spaces will be created alongside soft-edged and highly textured Contemporary rooms.

THEME KITCHENS
AND BATHROOMS

To help you sort through all of these periods, the following chart groups popular looks into broad categories. Such groupings may help organize your portfolio or picture file.

American Classic Rustic	Traditional (Country, Colonial)
	Shaker
	Arts & Crafts (Prairie Style, Bungalow Style)
	Rustic Americana (Southwestern, Spanish Mission, Lodge)
American Classic Formal	Traditional – Georgian
	Traditional – Federal
	Victorian
European Classic Rustic	English Country
	French Country
	Italian Tuscan
	Scandinavian Country
European Classic Formal	Biedermeier/French Empire
Modern/Contemporary Styling	Artisan Craftsman
	East Meets West
	Urban Contemporary
	Mid-Century Modernism

A review of the decorative elements of specific themed interiors follows. Note in particular the series of kitchen drawings beginning with Figure 5.1 on page 110. To illustrate how to achieve various theme effects using a variety of decorative and architectural details, the same kitchen plan is presented throughout this chapter with different theme variations. Focusing on how the details alone vary in the same kitchen will help clarify the role of decorative elements in creating a cohesive theme.

AMERICAN CLASSIC RUSTIC

American Traditional – American Country – 1620-1725 (or Colonial)

Historical Overview: American Country style is based on early American Colonial influences in the Northeast. Handcrafted simplicity is the hallmark of American Country: turned wood posts, straight lines, square shapes. This style features sturdy, rugged and crudely constructed elements. The pineapple motif is often used in hammered metal accents or stenciling patterns. Because of the rustic details, it is a very informal setting. The typical Colonial home combined rustic hand-made furnishings created here in the New World, with perhaps an occasional grand piece the family brought with them. Our early Colonists were proud of their possessions and displayed them. Open shelving is almost always seen in Colonial homes.

Cabinetry/Millwork: Use maple, pine, oak, birch, cherry and fruitwoods in natural or light finishes. Finish cabinets in solid colors, or feature faux finishes on the woodwork, as well. Stile-and-rail flat panel doors, butted board doors, or doors that include beaded board center panels are appropriate. Because of the rustic nature of this period, the door styling is simple. A corner cupboard is very appropriate, as is a table island or sideboard-type of cabinet accent piece.

Hardware: Use decorative brass with ceramic inlays, wrought iron, copper, oil-rubbed bronze, antique brass hardware, or rustic finishes.

Countertops: Use tile, square-edged solid surface materials, wood-trimmed laminate countertops, natural granite, slate or soapstone.

Colors: Extensive use of the primary colors—red, blue and yellow— reflects original dye colors. Alternatively, use muted tones so the colors appear as if they were applied years ago. Small patterns reflect the hand-woven nature of the textiles from this period.

Surfaces:

- **Floors:** Natural, rugged materials (real or simulated), such as wood plank, brick or rustic tile.

- **Walls:** Plaster walls, painted white or off-white. Beaded-board, patterned wall covering or wainscoting works well.

- **Ceilings:** Plaster ceiling, painted white or off-white with hand-hewn beams or wood ceiling.

Accents: Wrought iron and pewter metals, hand-made rugs. For an Old World look, the cabinetry should have a furniture or freestanding appearance, rather than the totally integrated look found in contemporary interiors.

Figure 5.1 *American Colonial Kitchen* Arched brick on the island ends and the wall, along with rugged beams and wood plank floors all contribute to the Colonial feel of this kitchen. (Courtesy of Don O'Connor, Wood-Mode Inc.)

Figure 5.2 *American Country Potting Room*
The rusticated antique beams, glazed finish, and modern interpretation of an old-fashioned porcelain sink create a country environment. (Courtesy of Wood-Mode Inc.)

Figure 5.3 *American Colonial Kitchen*
The wide plank floor and extensive use of beaded board cabinetry are appropriate for this log cabin Colonial-styled home. (Courtesy of Corsi Cabinet Company. Photography by Robert Millman Photography)

American Shaker

Historical Overview: "Shaker styling" is a term used in Europe, as well as North America, to define a beautifully executed, but severe in sensitivity and simple in detail, woodworking styling that is attributed to the craftspeople of the Shaker villages located in the Northeastern part of the United States. This was a religious sect known as the "Shakers" because of the activities the group engaged in during religious ceremonies. One of the tenets of this religion was celibacy: although the followers actively adopted children to continue the community, the last Shaker village closed in the early 20th Century.

The Shakers believed an important part of celebrating God was to always be busy and active in worthwhile tasks and to demand the best of oneself in the way one lived, as well as in the products created. The Shakers' homes were really dormitories—with men living in one and women in the other—and, therefore, were designed with multipurpose rooms. Chairs hung on pegs along the outer walls so floor space was available for other activities.

The design elements detailed under American Colonial Rustic are appropriate in Shaker design, with a focus on simplicity of detail and refinement of craftsmanship.

Cabinetry/Millwork: Use stile-and-rail recessed panel door with a plain inset, or flat panel door with lip construction; simple outside edge detail. Cherry and maple woods used extensively. Some figured wood, such as bird's-eye maple or tiger maple, used as well. Waxed or oiled warm-medium range wood tones. Occasionally, some of the woodwork, such as the window frames, peg rail, skirting or beaded board wall system, may be painted one of the Shaker colors detailed below.

Hardware and Accessories: Shaker artisans made a large variety of woodturnings for everything from cabinet pulls to pegs for wall hanging systems. Therefore, wood pegs are most authentic. Simple metal or hand-forged finishes are acceptable.

Countertops: Use square-edged solid surfaces, slate, soapstone, granite and limestone.

Colors: The Shaker dwellings were inevitably white plaster, against which a set range of colors were used in both paint and textiles. The distinctive color palette made use of the dyes and pigments from the clays and plants around them, ranging from pinky tones and terra cotta earth shades, through yellow ochre and olive green, to greenish blues and denim.

Surfaces:

- **Floors:** Typically, floors are varnished timber or wood, in some cases stone. Simple woven wood or rag rugs were laid on top of these hard surface floors.

- **Walls:** Painted or finished off-white or in earth tone colors. Typically, tall beaded board wainscoting was used with pegs.

- **Ceilings:** Plaster ceilings, painted white or off-white. Beams could be introduced.

Accents: Needless to say, fabrics were hand-woven and were frequently plain, as the Shakers avoided pattern. However, to lend relief to the otherwise plain interiors, they often wove checked fabrics: miniature ginghams, window checks, or checks that incorporated more than one color.

Figure 5.4 *Shaker Kitchen*
The configuration of the pantry and desk cabinetry, and the simple shape of the hood and island toe kick are all hallmarks of Shaker style. (Courtesy of Don O'Connor, Wood-Mode Inc.)

Figure 5.5 *Shaker Kitchen*
The simple pine cabinets, porcelain vessel sink with bridge faucet and reproduction floor set the stage for this Shaker kitchen. The wall-hung peg rack is a signature design element from Shaker villages. The wood countertop and matte finished black surface are also reminiscent of simple finishes. (Courtesy of Wood-Mode Inc.)

Arts & Crafts (Prairie Style, Bungalow Style) – 1880-1930

Historical Overview: The history of Arts & Crafts is grounded in craftsmen in both England and North America incensed by the lack of quality found in early machine-made furnishings. As the Industrial Revolution caused families to leave their rural settings and move to the cities, living accommodations were difficult and lives harsh. Decorative articles mass-produced for the emerging working class were shoddy and poorly made. The Arts & Crafts followers believed that by returning to an appreciation for finely crafted objects, a return to rural values would be possible. The simplicity and craftsmanship of the Shaker style and pre-industrial Japanese art were prized and collected. The Swedish Country style has many parallels to the Arts & Crafts movement as well. The underlying emphasis is simplicity of line, geometric ornamentation and handcrafted elegance.

Emerging out of the Arts & Crafts styling, yet retaining its basic tenets, is what is known as "The Prairie School of Design"—founded by a group of Chicago area artists who based their ideas and principals on early 1889 – 1910 work of Frank Lloyd Wright.

As an outgrowth of the Craftsman Era, Wright created homes that integrated the surrounding landscape, creating some of the most famous residences in North America. His strong Midwestern roots led to Prairie homes appropriate for cold winters with low roofs, long overhangs and intricate, hand-made, leaded-glass windows used in place of drapes. In contrast, California bungalow homes were (the exception is the architecture of Green and Green in Pasadena, California) catalog-ordered homes. These houses demonstrated an appreciation for the millwork and architectural detailing of the Midwestern masters by creating smaller scale and simplified molding details.

Cabinetry/Millwork: Plain, solid-wood furniture arranged in a functional manner. The furniture is large in scale, simple in design, and constructed of oak. Great care was taken to showcase the grain of the wood, the methods of joinery and hardware. Arts & Crafts designs often use cherry in place of oak today.

Hardware: Almost any brushed finish or metal, other than brass, works well. Intricately patterned metal work provides an authentic accent.

Countertops: Materials and other surface areas emphasize the inherent natural qualities, i.e., the strength of natural stone, the depth of highly glazed, multi-colored porcelain pottery, and the matte finish of rough earthenware-type materials.

Colors: Warm colors, golden yellow, soft green. Colors based on natural dyes, such as earth tones drawn from Indigo blue. Greens from every hue drawn from nature.

Surfaces:

- **Floor:** Plain or geometric patterns used in slate, tile or wood would be appropriate. Consider introducing American Indian patterns or other handcrafted items. In this style, true linoleum or vinyl in vintage patterns in matte finishes would be very authentic as well.

- **Walls:** Typical fabrics and wallcoverings are leather, wood and linen in solid colors and block printed cotton with stylized floral patterns and strong geometric repeats.

- **Ceiling:** Decorative light fixtures, stained glass shades from the Tiffany era, simple glass Mission pieces or decorative Art Nouveau pieces all blend beautifully.

Accents: Adjacent furniture pieces are always welcome in an Arts & Crafts room. Shaker baskets and Japanese ceramic and metal crafts would certainly be appropriate.

Figure 5.6 *Arts & Crafts Kitchen*
Woodworking details that feel
handcrafted, such as on the base of the
island, plus the decorative glass in the
cabinets, and the pattern on the soffit
and the light fixtures create an Arts
& Crafts room. (Courtesy of Don
O'Connor, Wood-Mode Inc.)

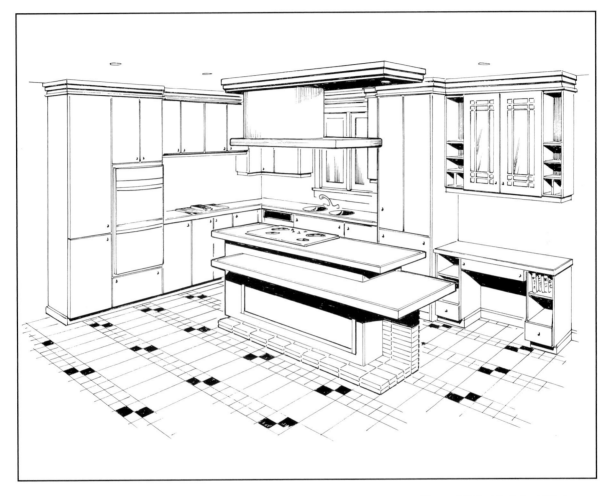

Figure 5.7 *Prairie School Kitchen*
The strong horizontal lines and the
geometric, but complex, patterns are
indicative of Prairie styling. (Courtesy
of Don O'Connor, Wood-Mode Inc.)

Figure 5.8 *Arts & Crafts Kitchen*
An Arts & Crafts kitchen is beautifully
executed in a natural cherry finish.
The woodworking design on the hood
is a major focal point. The appreciation
for nature is introduced in the fern tile
mural behind the cooking surface. The
cabinet doors are hand-crafted with
walnut butterfly joints highlighted in
key doors and panels. The design
detailing includes reproduction Arts &
Crafts cabinet hardware. (Courtesy of
Jennifer Gilmer, CKD – Chevy Chase,
Maryland. Photography by Bob Narod)

Rustic Americana (Southwestern, Spanish Mission, Lodge)

Historical Overview: Rustic Americana stretches from the sun-drenched desert of the Southwest, to the lodges of the Adirondacks in New York. These styles are grounded in the philosophy of hand craftsmanship, but are much more rugged in their execution and simplicity. They often include sun-baked desert colors, soft edges on heavily textured finishes and geometric patterns based on traditional Navajo Indian prints, with all materials and surfaces being hand-hewn in feel. Southwestern themes are more rusticated than Spanish Mission styling because of the American Indian influence.

The Spanish Mission styling shares many details with a Southwestern room but is more refined using metals more extensively and geometric patterns in woodwork. Patterns in materials (such as tiles) are influenced by the Moorish design aesthetic taken from Spain by Colonists to Mexico and then reinterpreted by settlers in California.

The Lodge look is based on Western ranch building materials and methods: log cabins with leather furniture accented by naturalistic patterns and native geometric woven designs.

Cabinetry/Millwork: Walnut, pine, oak. Very rustic cabinet detailing. Doors with turned posts. Stile-and-rail doors with curved or square top. Plank door styles, or square raised or recessed panel designs work. Cherry cabinets could be used as long as the style is very simple. Cabinet finishes can be whitewash, pickled, natural or light tones. Hand-carved details in simple naturalistic motifs accentuate this space.

Hardware: Rustic metals, wood, wrought iron, pewter are all appropriate.

Countertops: Countertops need to be natural and heavy in appearance and texture, and matte in finish. Wood, slate, soapstone, ceramic tile are appropriate.

Colors: White, off-white or neutral base color with warm, sun-baked color accents; grayed tones are also excellent accents.

Surfaces:

- **Floors:** Generally random patterned flagstone, slate, or wide random plank distressed wood floor.

- **Walls:** All surfaces are simple in finish; oftentimes, having almost a sense of a Colonial whitewash finish.

- **Ceilings:** White or soft neutral colors with dark, rough, heavy beams.

Accents: The motif, in any pattern, is typically naturalistic. Reproduction animal pelts, antlers, baskets, fishing gear, saddles, landscape paintings, horticultural prints, etc. all have a sense of a rustic homestead. Wrought iron and pounded brass metals, succulent and cacti greenery, natural fiber, nubby area carpets in solid colors or with Navajo Indian patterns, leather or twig furniture, and heavy pottery add detailing. Avoid accents that are imitations of traditional Indian artwork, or items that have a "Decorator Catalog" image. This theme is susceptible to becoming an overdone cliché of a beautiful style.

Figure 5.9 *Southwestern Dining Room Setting*
The angled plaster fireplace, introduction of ornate rusticated corbel pieces in the table, candelabra, chandelier and mantel candles support the carved detailing on the cabinets in this Southwestern room. (Courtesy of Catherine Dulacki, CKD – Denver, Colorado. Photography by Michael Stillman)

Figure 5.10 *Spanish Mission Kitchen*
The plaster curved arched wall openings of this kitchen
define the theme. (Courtesy of Raymond Kranz – La Jolla,
California)

AMERICAN CLASSIC FORMAL

American Traditional – American Georgian – 1725-1790

Historical Overview: The American Georgian style developed logically under King George of England (ca 1714 – 1810) and spread to North America with Colonists. Work by designers such as Chippendale, Hepplewhite and Sheraton characterized the style at its best. Georgian is a formal style with classical ties, so symmetry is important. Within these designs, molding details resulting in grand friezes, cornices, pillars and pilasters are important. Classical designs such as dentil, egg-and-dart, and Greek key are seen in many of the molding details. Carved corbels, brackets and appliqués or inlays of acanthus leaf and leafy garlands are also incorporated. The use of moldings and paneling are a key element to this style. Scalloped shell motif is seen in furniture detailing. And delicate curves and soft lines are also trademarks. A formal look and quality craftsmanship are hallmarks of this more refined interior.

Cabinetry/Millwork: Use mahogany, walnut, cherry and maple. Stile-and-rail doors with solid raised panels or flat panel doors with applied square molding and detailed panel edging. Painted cabinet finishes or lightly glazed painted finishes reflect the woodwork of the time.

Hardware: Brass, antique brass, copper, pewter are all appropriate.

Countertops: Wood-edged countertops or solid surface material with formal, routed edges. Hand-painted tiles are effective. Granite or marble both work well in these formal rooms.

Colors: Black (Oriental influence), red, green, blue; intense colors are used. Tints and tones may also be featured.

Surfaces:

- **Floors:** Plank or parquet flooring, Oriental area rugs, hall runners and area carpets work well in small bathrooms.

- **Walls:** Painted, paneled walls or wood wainscoting. Small patterned wallcovering.

- **Ceilings:** Plaster with ceiling crown molding. No heavy beams that contrast with ceiling.

Accents: Gold, brass or antique brass metals are used. Furniture pieces add authenticity.

Figure 5.11 *American Georgian Kitchen*
The broken pediment over the refrigerator, the use of fluted columns, and the formal, not random, floor pattern all bring the Georgian flavor to this kitchen. (Courtesy of Don O'Connor, Wood-Mode Inc.)

Figure 5.12 *American Georgian Cabinet*
The formal detailing on this china cabinet adjacent to a kitchen creates a Georgian feel with its columns, classic proportions, woodworking detailing and brass hardware. (Courtesy of Karen Williams – New York, New York. Photography by Peter Leach.)

Figure 5.13 *American Georgian Bathroom*
Once again, the inset, intricately detailed cabinet accented by carved corbels create a very formal American Georgian setting. The mirrors continue the formalness of the space. (Courtesy of Jeannie Fulton – Ridgewood, New Jersey)

American Traditional – American Federal – 1795-1830

Historical Overview: Style inspired by the English furniture makers Fife, Hepplewhite and Sheraton, and influenced by French Empire. Federal is the American adaptation of French Empire. Therefore, the Napoleonic eagle became the eagle of liberty. Duncan Fife is the most famous Federal furniture designer. His work—or careful reproductions—clearly defines this style. It is reserved and dignified in mood, classical because of geometric patterns seen throughout this type of space.

It is the most formal and dignified of all American interiors. Classical detailing, such as Greek key and fret patterns, predominate.

Cabinetry/Millwork: Mahogany, walnut, cherry. Inset doors with classic Greek Key molding or intricate, applied molding. Stile-and-rail door with curved raised panel, classic, white finishes on cabinets.

Hardware: Formal hardware: polished brass can be used in this setting. Intricate metal work is also appropriate.

Countertops: Laminate or solid surface countertops with detailed edges. Natural stone in a polished finish. Delicate and patterned tiles are excellent accents.

Colors: Red, blue, yellow, green and some pastels.

Surfaces:

- **Floor:** Wood parquet patterns are ideal. Simple square vinyl or tiles are also acceptable. Dark floors work well with white cabinets.

- **Walls:** Plaster walls with elaborate door and window moldings.

- **Ceiling:** Plaster with ceiling crown moldings.

Accents: Brass and gold metals to trim countertops, fine porcelain, detailed glass and muntin cabinet doors are all appropriate.

Figure 5.14 *Federal Kitchen*
With a tailored feel, this Federal kitchen includes dentil molding on the hood and a furniture leg-inspired detail on the island. (Courtesy of Don O'Connor, Wood-Mode Inc.)

Figure 5.15 *Federal Kitchen*

While white is seen so often, this soft yellow kitchen is definitely an American Federal setting because of its Classic Greek molding and intricate applied molding. Note the dropped detail on the pilasters at each end of the extended island: they are actually reproduction pieces from a mantel in the Winterthur Museum in Winterthur, Delaware. (Courtesy of Ellen Cheever, CMKBD, ASID – Wilmington, Delaware and Sub-Zero Freezer Co., Inc.)

Figure 5.16 *Federal Butler's Pantry*
Classic white cabinetry and glass
doors seen against an old pine floor set
the stage for this Federal room.
(Courtesy of Jere Bowden, CKD –
Atlanta, Georgia. Photography by
John Umberger Photography)

Victorian – 1830-1919

Historical Overview: The Victorian Era is named after Queen Victoria of England and coincides with the introduction of the Industrial Revolution. Queen Victoria was an enthusiastic amateur artist and decorator, personally designing her palace at Balmoral using light wood tones, pale blue and green accents, and plenty of glass to let the light in. Doesn't sound very Victorian? The Victorian style that is typically seen in interiors today is extremely detailed because of the preponderance of machine-made woodworking, dark and somber in color tones with heavy wood grains. Medieval motifs such as stylized floral patterns, filigree, lancet arched windows and leaded glass panes create the intricately detailed themes popular in Victorian interiors.

Cabinetry/Millwork: Heavy dark woods are typically used such as mahogany, blackened oak, walnut, satinwood or rosewood. Raised panel doors, multiple panel doors, heavily stacked moldings and hand-carved appliqués or inlays would be appropriate.

Hardware: Ornate polished brass, ceramic or marble inset with inlays are appropriate.

Countertops: Wood, marble, granite and ceramic tiles. Consider 3" x 6" running bond brick backsplash and wainscot materials.

Colors: Very dark, low intensity colors are used. Combination of olive green, black, burgundy and golden tones can easily be placed together—all in one room.

Surfaces:

- **Floors:** Patterned floors—in reproduction linoleum and vinyl, or marble, limestone or terrazzo work for recreating this style.

- **Walls:** Exotic Oriental or historical themes on imported wallcoverings. Flocked silk damask and other heavy materials used as wallcoverings.

- **Ceilings:** Typically painted, and continue down the wall to a molding that was used to hang pictures so the hardware did not damage the wall covering.

Accents: Heavy fabric window treatments, very intricately detailed furniture, Oriental-type carpets. Very elaborate curved cabinet styling. Beveled glass used in mullion doors.

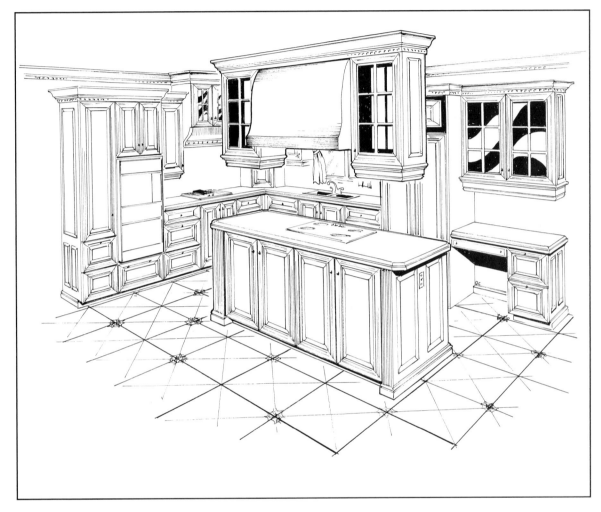

Figure 5.17 *Victorian Kitchen*
The elegantly shaped hood, highly detailed floor, and heavy miter-framed door style all contribute to the Victorian feel of this kitchen. (Courtesy of Don O'Connor, Wood-Mode Inc.)

Figure 5.18 *Victorian Kitchen*
The antique reproduction appliances,
light fixture and ceiling covering are
reminiscent of those materials found
during Victorian times. The cabinet
detailing would be appropriate in
many settings: in this example, it
provides an elegant backdrop for the
highly styled appliances. (Courtesy
of Decora Cabinets, Designed by
Heather Dilger – Jeffersonville,
Indiana. Photography by Bob Hower)

Figure 5.19 *Victorian Bathroom*
The carvings featured on the vanity, combined with the reproduction Victorian light fixtures and ornate mirror, create a Victorian room. (Courtesy of Peter Ross Salerno, CMKBD – Wyckoff, New Jersey)

EUROPEAN CLASSIC RUSTIC

English Country

Historical Overview: Don O'Connor, of Wood-Mode Inc., explained English Country interiors well when he said, "Country English became popular in the US in the early 90s, maybe as a reaction against the European look. It's less an acknowledged style than a clever concoction of 19th Century English design elements, some of them indeed from rural interiors. Its popularity is waning somewhat, not only, I suspect, because of budget, but also because owners have belatedly discovered that, absent a maid, all that open work and detailing means a lot of upkeep! It is a contradiction in terms, but the feeling ought to be casually elaborate and formal, as if the owners were too rich to be concerned with anything as bourgeois as coordination."

English Country styling details are drawn from the small cottages as well as the grand country manor houses seen throughout the UK. With the English preference for Georgian styling and Gothic details, it is a heavy style with a great deal of woodworking prevalent. A square line dominates the cabinet shapes. However, curved shapes and lines can be seen in the architectural elements of the room.

Cabinetry/Millwork: Oak, cherry, mahogany, pine in natural or medium stains along with painted finishes. "Paint dragging" or special "antiquing" finishing processes enhance stile-and-rail flat or raised panel door styles. Inset doors have heavy applied moldings. Panel doors with small symmetrically arranged repetitive raised sections are signature features of English rooms. Beaded board interiors of open shelf units and panels installed between cabinets with detailed face edges of a "pilaster" are commonly seen. Open filigree valances, spindle dish cabinets, cabinetry with multiple drawers and half or full turnings set the stage for this room. Turned posts, heavy molding and geometric or stylized cut-outs in panels are all appropriate architectural elements of the space.

Hardware: Copper, brass, antique brass, porcelain accents, pewter or nickel finishes are appropriate.

Countertops: All available counter surfaces work well in an English Country environment. Because intricate woodworking is often showcased in these interiors, the countertop detailing remains fairly simple. Dramatic detailing may be featured on the backsplash. Proportionately, consider oversized countertop edges, island counter shape details or ceramic stone backsplash as key design elements.

Colors: Primary accents are appropriate. Painted cabinet finishes are generally pastel.

Surfaces:

- **Floors:** Tile, brick, stone or wood patterns in reproduction or natural patterns.

- **Walls:** Heavily textured stucco walls. Tongue and groove wainscoting in beaded board or with stile-and-rail raised panel sections, finished with a chair rail, is effective. Heavy crown moldings and baseboards are frequently used.

- **Ceilings:** Hand-hewn beams to match or contrast with cabinets or boxed beams to match ceiling are used.

Accents: Flowers are seen everywhere. The room should have a definite tie to the garden and countryside beyond the back door. Use a collection of floral fabrics throughout the space. Muntin doors with fabric gathers, or shelves with linen and lace doilies add a special touch. An English armoire might house the pantry or the refrigeration equipment. Architectural millwork details are an integral part of an English space—and many include a large, oversized hood.

Figure 5.20 *English Country Kitchen*
Cabinetry has the feel of pieces of
furniture pushed together. Other
English Country details are bun feet
and corner cutouts on the island,
breakfront with bead board and
irregular tile floors. (Courtesy of Don
O'Connor, Wood-Mode Inc.)

Figure 5.21 *English Country Kitchen*
English Country kitchens can be rusticated or formal—this unfitted example is clearly from the English countryside. Glazed pine is the featured wood with open spaces framed by crafted carved turnings. Woodworking details reminiscent of those that might be crafted from artisans in small villages are suggested in this cabinetry, and supported by the well-worn table and chairs in the foreground. Very English—the plate rail above the sink. (Courtesy of Rutt HandCrafted Cabinetry. Photography by Don Pearse Photography)

Figure 5.22 *English Country Kitchen*
A classic formal English Country kitchen features white cabinets combined with pine island chairs with sophisticated turnings. The running bond tile splash and introduction of marble, combined with the nickel finishes on the hardware, are the details surrounding this English Bespoke Kitchen. (Courtesy of Christopher Peacock, Bespoke English Cabinetry)

French Country

Historical Overview: "French Country" is a name used to describe a home in the provinces of France—therefore, we could call it French Provincial. (Professional designers typically do not use that term because it is too often associated with overly detailed bedroom suites.) This style is reflective of homes dotting the French countryside, which were furnished by prosperous farmers with furnishings and room settings initially inspired by the Parisian Court's high style, but were simplified and made much less pretentious by regional workmen. However, French Country rooms are sophisticated and do include a great deal of detail.

These rooms—like many European country settings—have a sense of evolving. They are a collection of patterns, colors and materials that please the homemaker, having been gathered by the family over time. The rooms are relatively light in color and have a feminine sense, with curved lines dominating. Simple lines are acceptable in a Peasant French atmosphere, more complex arrangements work well in more refined rooms.

Cabinetry/Millwork: Walnut, pine, cherry and fruit woods in natural and light finishes with some aging, distressing or artistic enhancement. Colored surfaces are also appropriate in Country French. Mixing colors and wood finishes in an unfitted environment reflects the casual style of a provincial French home.

Hardware: May be bronze, copper, iron or pewter. Hammered surfaces are acceptable—but polished are more historically valid. Oversized hardware—long metal hinges, for example—and fanciful hand-wrought details can be employed in these rooms.

Countertops: Solid surface, quartz, natural or man-made marble, natural stone, ceramic tile or laminate countertops with detailed edges can all be effectively used. Solid surface counters may feature delicate tile inlays or gently sculptured edge treatments. Keep ceramic tile smooth in texture and match grout colors on counter or splash areas. Decorative laminate counters combine well with wood or faux wood front edges and ceramic tile backsplash areas.

Colors: Country French rooms oftentimes contrast warm and cool color groupings. For example, wood tones can be warm with cooler accessory colors or the reverse. Pastels are also appropriate in a French setting, as are the more vibrant colors and patterns seen in the French faience patterned fabric so famous from the south of France.

Surfaces:

- **Floors:** Heavy, rustic materials are appropriate. Brick, limestone, terra cotta quarry tiles. Hardwood parquet or plank patterns in reproduction or natural products.

- **Walls:** Painted plaster walls or floral wallcovering with small patterns. Delicate crown moldings and beaded baseboards are effective in these spaces. Faux finished decorative treatments work well in a Country French setting because they simulate aged wood finishes.

- **Ceilings:** Boxed beams finished to match or contrast with cabinets or ceiling finish. Beaded or random plank ceilings reflect the rustic sense of a French Country setting.

Accents: Metals, fine porcelain pieces called "French faience," curved mullion doors with beveled glass, delicately patterned fabrics associated with the South of France. Lace fabric on shelves inside cabinets with glass doors can add a special touch. Incorporate a mantel hood area or a fireplace. Large windows should be tall and narrow with rectangular hardware and a deep sill created in reality or as a visual effect.

When looking at accent furniture pieces, you can increase the formality of the room or support the rustic setting by recommending the "right" type of regional pieces. Provincial furniture was made by highly skilled chair and cabinetmakers from cities near Paris. French Country furniture—rustic pieces—were made for farmhouses in Normandy, hunting lodges in Burgundy and the modest cottages in the Ile-de-France. The forms of these pieces usually mirrored Parisian styles but were shorn of excess and ornamentation.

Figure 5.23 *French Country Kitchen*
Curves on the furniture-type island, repeated on the glass insets of the cabinet doors, contribute to the French Country design, along with mullioned doors and an elaborate shaded light fixture. (Courtesy of Don O'Connor, Wood-Mode Inc.)

Figure 5.26 *French Country Vanity*
A Queen Anne vanity with carved
furniture legs and a carved apron
rendered in an antique cherry are
combined with detailed brass pulls
and faucetry in this French Country
bath. (Courtesy of Heritage Custom
Cabinetry)

Tuscan

Historical Overview: Another European design setting is found in the Tuscan portion of Italy. Its look is quite different from the English Country or French Country. The major difference is the extensive use of arch openings and/or details in heavily plastered, oversized rooms. The delicate, feminine refinement of Country French is absent, as is the heavy Gothic detailing of an English environment. Rather, the dark woods balance with soft-edged stone surfaces and vibrantly painted tile murals. The overall room feels like an Italian villa atop a hill in the Tuscan countryside. The look of this room is extravagant and exuberant—but it does still have some discipline.

Cabinetry/Millwork: Oak, pine, mahogany—any heavy wood with a strong grain works well in an Italian Country setting. Cherry is probably too refined. If painted finishes are used, they are definitely distressed and worn through. Arched doors, flat panel doors and the introduction of wire or lattice within the doors help to establish the Italian theme. A combination of plaster structures and cabinetry works well because many Tuscan houses have open niches in plaster walls, backsplash shelves created from plaster, and a plaster fireplace or a plaster hood as part of the cabinetry to the ceiling.

Hardware: Rustic metals and crackled finishes on porcelain are excellent hardware selections. Italian settings support extensive use of metals and metallic surfaces above and beyond hardware. Brackets to support countertop overhangs, freestanding rack-type display units, overhead hanging systems or wall-mounted shelving all can be used.

Countertops: Once again, most available counter surfaces work well. The more rustic, the better. Textured and patterned solid surfaces, soapstone and active granites and marbles are all excellent choices. In non-water areas, heavy wood tops might work as well.

Colors: Sun-washed warm colors in yellows, oranges and reds balanced by blues and greens work well. In addition to these warm tones, olive green and terra cotta combined with wrought iron, copper and verdigris metallic have an "Italian" sense to them.

Surfaces:

- **Floors:** Any rustic, hardy material—tile, stone, wood—can be used. The room would be greatly enhanced by the addition of an area rug.

147

- **Walls:** Textured walls with a layered finish are typically used. Wood wainscoting is not appropriate in an Italian villa room—but a tile wainscoting would be great.

- **Ceilings:** Cabinetry with open space above is an excellent choice. Keep the molding up around the ceiling. Beams work in any country environment, but a faux finish feeling is also appropriate in an Italian setting.

Accents: Stucco/textured/plaster sections within the space combined with oversized windows. Mixing furniture in the space to display Italian pottery is appropriate. Long refractory or harvest tables in the space and a collection of mismatched chairs work well.

Figure 5.27 *Italian Tuscan Kitchen* Hardy materials and an emphasis on pattern such as the lattice cabinet doors contribute to the Tuscan style. Note the heavy ceramic tile behind the hood, the rusticated beams and the heavy legs on the island and desk. (Courtesy of Don O'Connor, Wood-Mode Inc.)

Figure 5.28 *Italian Tuscan Kitchen*
The Tuscan countryside is rich in sun-drenched colors and textured materials. This kitchen is rich in details found in the Italian countryside. The carved grape motif molding around the hood sets the stage. The designer wisely used a plaster hood, as opposed to a wood hood, to introduce the finishes typical of Italian villas. Oversized, bold, heavily distressed woodworking details in the cabinetry continue the theme. (Courtesy of Sally Ann Sullivan, CKD – Tulsa, Oklahoma and Wm Ohs Inc.)

Figure 5.29 *Italian Tuscan Kitchen*
Light glazed cabinets and dark woods are finishes often used alone—or combined in Tuscan kitchens. Maple is used here on the island combined with the light glazed cabinetry along the perimeter of the room. The arched transom windows over the doors are echoed in the oven tall unit which repeats the shape seen in the hand carvings at the end of the island. (Courtesy of Patricia Mauro, CKD, CBD—Milford, Connecticut)

Scandinavian Country

Historical Overview: Swedish Country style, like French and English, is more rustic than the royal court style featured in the aristocracy's homes in these countries. The long, dark northern nights have led many Swedish interiors to feature lighter colors and simpler details. Available materials in the Swedish environment are used instead of costly and rare ones. Because the country is heavily forested with softwoods, the rooms feature simple woods and hand-made materials. Eclectic styling is often seen as an integral part of Swedish homes. If one studies the Shaker villages of New England and Swedish Country, there are definite similarities, with the difference in color tone being one of the only striking differences. The Shaker village used more American primary colors, while the Swedish used light, pastel tones.

Cabinetry/Millwork: Pine and other tightly grained woods are appropriate. Painted or pale limed finishes or natural finishes on wood are useful. An uncluttered look is an important hallmark of Swedish Country styling, with a focus on the functional storage provided. Open shelving, mixed with dressers, sideboards and other furniture pieces converted to kitchen use, is appropriate. Simple frame and recess panel door styles with delicate, simple moldings based on classical motifs are also suitable.

Hardware: Simplicity, symmetry and usefulness are the key to hardware selections. Porcelain, wood, pewter all are appropriate.

Countertops: Although wood would be the most realistic, wood printed laminate, rustic stone or tile is also appropriate. A quartz material would be an excellent choice. Granite or marble would not be appropriate in this type of room.

Colors: Pattern is used sparingly, usually woven checks and stripes or delicate floral prints, always understated. White, blue, pale green, yellow, red and ecru are very typical, with touches of brown or bottle green.

Surfaces:

- **Floors:** Wood floors that are scrubbed, lime-washed or finished with a gray tone are appropriate. Rag rugs and runners in red, gray, cream or pale blue work well.

- **Walls:** Stenciling and faux painting may be used on the soft tone-on-tone pastel finishes on the walls.

- **Ceilings:** Simple painted ceilings in pastel shades are appropriate.

EUROPEAN CLASSIC FORMAL – 1820-1850

Biedermeier/French Empire

Historical Overview: Empire was a decorative style under Napoleon I which was classically based and borrowed heavily on Imperial Roman icons such as eagles and fasces (fasces are a bundle of rods with an ax with projecting blade mixed among the rods), as well as Egyptian motifs. The Empire lines are masculine and dramatic. It is a style of the city, formal and austere. It is rarely selected for a kitchen or bathroom design.

More likely to be used is the German/Austrian version of French Empire, called "Biedermeier." It flourished from 1820 to about the middle of 1850, and has recently been revived because of the warm fruit woods and cherry woods used and its detailing, which makes it an interesting element in a Transitional room. A side note: the name is not of a famous architect. It grew out of a cartoon about a common man named "Papa Biedermeier" (an insult meaning a simple, unsophisticated man). The style is simplified, yet does use sophisticated geometric and classical forms. Of importance is the strong contrast between dark and pale woods and gilded accents, which are one of its hallmarks.

Cabinetry/Millwork: Clear wood, simple lines in maple, beech, ash, cherry with a beaded inset panel are the most popular styles. The bead may be finished black, as might other moldings and hardware selections. The moldings are simple in nature and have flowing lines. Consider an arched crown rather than one having a stepped ogee, for example.

Hardware: Traditional with linear detailing. Brass or bronze, black or other metal surfaces.

Countertops: Any of the popular countertop materials can be used in dark simple colors or deeper, formal tones.

Colors: Backdrop colors used in this room are subtle beiges, creams, vibrant yellows, blues, soft grays, aquamarine, sandstone and parchment with black and gilt accents.

Surfaces:

• **Floors:** A wood floor is the best selection. Consider bordering the floor with a darker wood.

• **Walls:** Vertical patterned wallcovering, faux, geometric-patterned finishes work well. Use of a border is appropriate.

• **Ceilings:** Painted, relatively simple ceilings work well.

Accents: This room is well suited for a table and chair in a Biedermeier or Empire style. Leather, woven textures, geometric prints all work well.

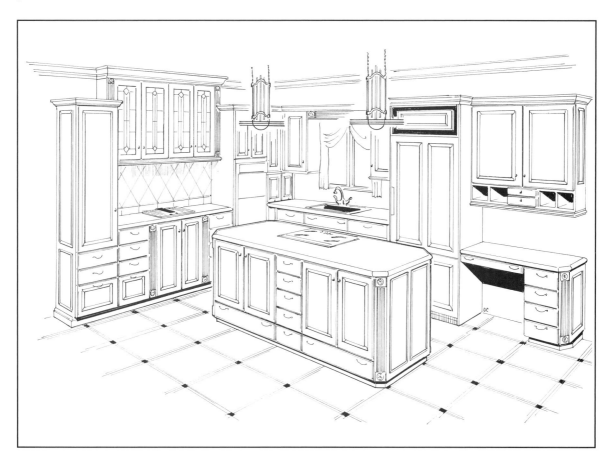

Figure 5.30 *Biedermeier Kitchen*
Very linear, this Biedermeier kitchen would most likely be designed with two different finishes and black details in the floor. Rosettes on the top and bottom of the fluted pilasters are another hallmark of this style. (Courtesy of Don O'Connor, Wood-Mode Inc.)

Figure 5.31 *Biedermeier-styled Entertainment Center*
Biedermeier styling is beautifully detailed in this display in an appliance
distributor's showroom. Ribbon-cut cherry veneer is used on the cabinetry
enhanced by the framing bead finished in black. The designer continues this
dramatic detailing in the chair and table base, as well as the artwork throughout
the space. (Courtesy of Jennifer Gilmer, CKD – Chevy Chase, Maryland)

Figure 5.32 *Biedermeier-styled Bathroom*
Bathrooms are far less dramatic than
kitchens—however, this bath at the
Kohler Design Center has a sense of
Biedermeier style and drama. A
Toulouse-Lautrec dancehall girl eyes
the visitor from the painting behind
the tub. The dramatic use of dark
finished woods, vibrant yellow towels
and furniture pieces suggest the drama
of Europe in the late 1800s. (Courtesy
of Gay Fly – Galveston, Texas)

DIVERSITY OF 21ST CENTURY CONTEMPORARY DESIGN

In the Introduction to this chapter, we differentiated "Modern," "Contemporary" and "International" designs over the last 90 years, dividing them into numerous categories. As we study interpretations of Contemporary more closely now, we will take a much broader eclectic view by considering four overall groupings of style aesthetics. One is not more correct than the others, none are more important than the other. Each is simply a different version of Contemporary design themes.

- **Artisan Crafted:** Based on an emerging reinterpretation of Arts & Crafts styling, the work of Frank Lloyd Wright and American Shaker simplicity. Today's inspired artisans are crafting Contemporary rooms (oftentimes labeled "Transitional") finding their spirit in the Arts & Crafts movement, but working hard to create a room appropriate for today's family.

- **East Meets West:** A sub-category within the first style group is "East Meets West." Asian Pacific sensibility is blending with North American and European design themes to create beautifully crafted, yet elegantly simple rooms. The Asian Pacific theme is global in its design interpretation, yet always based on the complex contradiction of dissimilar materials combined together, resulting in an environment rich in pattern interest and strongly emphasizing horizontal lineal interest.

- **Urban Contemporary:** The sophisticated preference for minimalism in materials and elements of the design solution. The evolution of the "Euro-look" and "High-Tech" look of the 1980s has been redefined by architects such as John Pawson in London, and is now defined as "Minimalism." Probably best executed by Italian and German industrial designers and furniture makers, it focuses on simplicity, yet provides great textural interest in the materials selected.

- **Mid-Century Modernism.** The return of design elements from past eras remains a perpetually hot trend—such is the case with today's interest in a "Retro" look kitchen. There are two distinctly different versions of Mid-Century Modernism. First is, a design discipline celebrating brightly colored new materials which were an extension of products that grew out of the chemistry world. Lightweight materials such as fiberglass, cast aluminum, acrylic and resin were used by noted designers to create interesting furniture pieces and accents. Color is used everywhere in this first version of Mid-Century Modernism. The second Mid-Century styling is directly linked to designs originated in Scandinavia. Designers Charles and Ray Eames led the way with a focus on natural woods such as teak and plywood combined with much softer, subtle colors such as faded chartreuse green, chestnut orange and willow yellow. Both interpretations of design from the 1950s provide excellent accents for an Urban Contemporary setting, or can certainly stand on their own.

These four variations are the basis for Contemporary styling today.

Artisan Crafted

Historical Overview: An emerging design trend today for modern settings is one that combines the sensitivity of Shaker styling, turn-of-the-century Arts & Crafts details and European ideas from Italy and Scandinavia. A good way to describe this type of interior is a "softer Contemporary." Naturalistic patterns and materials predominate throughout the space; for example, slate or limestone on the floor. However, these natural materials are combined with hard-edged surfaces such as stainless steel and colored cabinetry. These interiors are oftentimes inspired by Art Deco geometric symmetry, and most often are definitely eclectic environments.

Cabinetry/Millwork: Straight-grained woods predominate today. Oak is returning in popularity, maple in specialty cut woods, and cherry. Door styles can be flat slab doors, but stile-and-rail square edged, "Shaker-type" doors are also appropriate. Asymmetrically balanced door designs that introduce glass patterns or woodworking cutouts are also effective.

Hardware: Because this style pulls from the past, in addition to the popular brushed nickel and brushed stainless steel finishes in modern environments, pounded antiqued and distressed metals can also be used.

Countertops: Popular countertop materials work well: granite, quartz, solid surfaces, laminate. Some specialty counters that add texture—such as concrete surfaces—are also appropriate. Honed granites, soapstone and limestone are popular.

Colors: All colors from the color wheel can be used. Low intensity is preferable. Deep earthen porcelain colors seen in pottery from the Arts & Crafts period work well in these environments.

Surfaces:

- **Floors:** Wood, slate, stone, reintroduced original linoleum/vinyl or new vinyl patterns reminiscent of the past are all appropriate.

- **Walls:** Typically, textured walls—either plaster finished or faux finished—are appropriate. Little wallcovering.

- **Ceilings:** Painted, simple ceilings. These rooms benefit from unusual angled ceilings, skylights or other overhead architectural elements.

Accents: Furniture from the Arts & Crafts or Shaker period. The introduction of geometric woodworking details in partitions, columns or soffit work. Glass block, decorative legs.

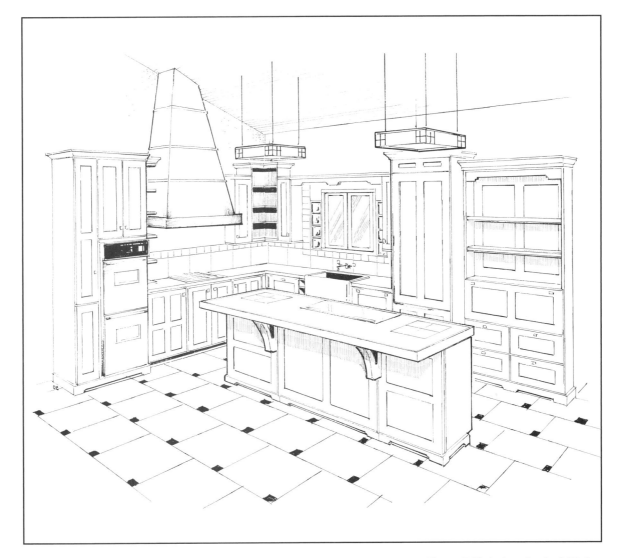

Figure 5.33 *Artisan-Inspired Kitchen That Includes Art Deco Details*
One-of-kind touches such as the hood and the light fixtures contribute Artisan touches to this kitchen, as do the corbel shapes. The overall sense is geometric. (Courtesy of Don O'Connor, Wood-Mode Inc.)

Figure 5.34 *Artisan Crafted Kitchen*
This elegant combination of stainless steel and natural finished maple—accented by a blue textured tile behind the cooking surface—suggests a space inspired by the "wabi-sabi" appreciation of the old. (Courtesy of Wood-Mode Inc.)

Figure 5.35 *Artisan Crafted Vanity Area*
The hand-crafted combination of stone, shaped glass and wood used by the designer is an excellent example of softer contemporary styling. The bath space is expanded by the use of large-scale neutral gray tiles on the floor accented by marble tiles on the wall. (Courtesy of Sally Power – San Francisco, California)

Figure 5.36 *Artisan Crafted Kitchen*
The cabinetry in this kitchen would support many different themes in design. The selection of furniture and accessories identifies it as an Artisan Crafted space. The lattice wood chair backs, pottery and artwork soften this Contemporary space. (Courtesy of Wood-Mode Inc.)

Figure 5.37 *Artisan Crafted Kitchen*
A traditional kitchen features many of the elements described as being reflective of an "artisan-crafted" kitchen. Note the custom turnings on the butcher block furniture piece placed adjacent to the island. The antique Oriental carpet runner introduced in the space continues this theme. Pottery used to accessorize the room provides a hand-crafted decorative piece as well. (Courtesy Jeannie Fulton – Ridgewood, New Jersey. Photography by Peter Rymwid.)

Figure 5.38 *Artisan Crafted Bathroom*
Introducing an unusual shaped mirror and detailed light fixture helps this
otherwise sleek Contemporary room have an Artisan sense to it. (Courtesy
of Marie A. Thompson, CKD, CBD – Redmond, Washington. Photography by
David Livingston)

Figure 5.39 *Artisan Crafted Bathroom*
The Arts & Crafts influence in this
bath is clearly seen in the light fixtures
and hardware selected for the space.
Oftentimes Artisan Crafted rooms
combine elements from the Arts &
Crafts movement, as well as Asian
design materials or geometric patterns.
(Courtesy of Jacqueline Balint, CKD –
Redondo Beach, California. Photography
by Larry A. Falke Photography)

East Meets West

Historical Overview: There is not a clear historic background to this style preference. It is more an emerging appreciation for the simplicity of Pacific Rim environments. In traditional Japanese design and its many interpretations, what designers admire are the restrained architecture and interiors focusing on presenting uncluttered elegance, which is rare in the global design world. Over the centuries, the Japanese have developed a unique design vocabulary focusing on quiet, unpretentious objects placed in interiors so they can be individually enjoyed and highly valued.

"The simplicity of Pacific Rim environments seems to be based on the ethic of creating beautiful things without getting caught up in the disparaging materialism that oftentimes surrounds creative acts," says Leonard Koran, the author of *Wabi-Sabi – for Artists, Designers, Poets & Philosophers*. In rooms inspired by Asian design, beautiful craftsmanship, simplicity of shape and the juxtaposition and resulting interplay between honest, dissimilar, natural materials are at the heart of the design. The style is pared down, not cold but soothing, not empty but uncluttered.

Cabinetry/Millwork: Straight-grained, simple doors with wood graining direction being either horizontal or vertical, or a combination of both. Cabinets are used to create unusual asymmetrical or angled shapes within the space. Oak, maple, cherry, recut or reconstituted veneers, and Western cedar are all appropriate in natural finishes. Oftentimes, a darker wood is combined with a lighter wood to create horizontal linear interest by the interplay of woods, rather than stacked or elaborate moldings. A combination of open shelves and enclosed storage is appropriate to maintain the light, airy sense of a Japanese environment.

Hardware: Either as unobtrusive as possible or a major element in the space, or a combination of both. Matte finished hardware predominates.

Countertops: Matte finished surfaces, such as concrete, stainless steel, granite, soapstone and wood are often used. The backsplash area may accent the overall horizontal line introduced in this design. Oversized, thicker counters and changes in counter heights are appropriate. Glass tiles for the backsplash are appropriate in this setting.

Colors: Natural colors (from the forest, sky or seaside) are all appropriate. A strong use of textured surfaces is typically seen as opposed to combinations of colors.

Surfaces:

- **Floors:** Concrete, wood or natural stone floors predominate.

- **Walls:** Textured faux finished walls, wood paneled walls (consider graining horizontally) or crisp, simply finished walls. Horizontal window designs are appropriate. Views to the outside garden greatly enhance a room inspired by the Pacific Rim.

- **Ceilings:** Simple, classic ceilings. A rustic beam ceiling also would be appropriate in this type of environment.

Accents: Stainless steel is an excellent accent material. Little ornamentation. Retro/Mid-Century Modern furniture works well.

Figure 5.40 *Pacific Rim Kitchen*
Characterized by a preponderance of linear, horizontal pattern, this Pacific Rim-inspired kitchen is more complex than it first appears. For example, the floor pattern is actually quite complicated. (Courtesy of Don O'Connor, Wood-Mode Inc.)

Figure 5.41 *Pacific Rim Kitchen*
The combination of rough and smooth
finishes is a highlight of this space.
Note the flooring combined with
the 4" x 4" glass tiles at the splash.
Asymmetrical balance is seen
throughout the custom cabinetry as
well. (Courtesy of Fu-Tung Cheng –
Berkeley, California. Photography by
Matthew Millman)

Figure 5.42 *East Meets West Bathroom*
The horizontal nature of the glass cloth wallpaper is repeated in the horizontal lines of the Shoji-type screen entry door. The stained concrete floor blends nicely with the pebble detail on the shower base. (Courtesy of Alan Hilsabeck, Jr., CKD, CBD, ASID – Dallas, Texas)

Figure 5.43 *East Meets West Bathroom* A major plumbing manufacturer created an Asian-inspired bath with the introduction of the long horizontal lines seen in the woodworking along the back wall. The accessorizing with the twigs in the vase and the soap dish complete the space. (Courtesy of American Standard, Inc.)

Figure 5.44 *East Meets West Bathroom* The sympathy between the Arts & Crafts movement and Asian design is seen in this bath with its hardware from the Arts & Crafts timeframe, yet its entry door and light fixtures are clearly inspired by the Japanese Shoji screen. These two styles live well together. (Courtesy of Jacqueline Balint, CKD – Redondo Beach, California. Photography by Larry A. Falke Photography)

Urban Contemporary

Historical Overview: For the last 20 years, "Contemporary" has typically been described as an emphasis on architectural shapes, with strong lineal interest created by blocks of space defined by the connected cabinet elements. Unadorned, structural materials are often featured (think of a New York City loft with its oversized windows and brick walls). Today's Urban Contemporary continues to have a sleek, simple architectural basis for this design.

Cabinetry/Millwork: Oak, teak, birch, maple. Most popular woods are appropriate. Straight grains prevail. In many of these rooms the cabinetry doors are not wood at all, but rather stainless steel, acrylic/polyester in gloss or matte finishes, or painted surfaces. Although most of the doors are slab doors, narrowly dimensioned stile-and-rail doors are also appropriate. Aluminum frame doors that feature frosted, ribbed or other patterned glass accent many of the designs.

Hardware: Typically chrome, stainless steel or nickel. Polished or brass is appropriate.

Countertops: Stainless steel, concrete, and natural stone are a great choice.

Colors: The only limiting factor is the designer's imagination. European designers often use large blocks of cabinetry in vibrant primary colors: blue, orange, red, lime green. Neutral colors in blacks and whites, blue-based gray or yellow "taupe" grays are extremely popular. Stainless steel is a key accent material, which "reads" gray as far as a color addition. An emerging popular color is a dark black-brown used on open-grained woods such as oak or ash.

Surfaces:

- **Floors:** In eclectic settings, the floor could be a worn wide-plank pine floor or a unique Wenge, dark floor. Alternatively, the floor could be almost a bleached, narrow plank maple floor. Vinyl floors are a possibility, as is concrete or cork flooring.

- **Walls:** Typically painted simple colors. Brick is an appropriate material installed in 3" x 6" or 4" x 8" sizes in a running bond pattern.

- **Ceilings:** Simple painted ceilings enhanced, once again, by open beams, skylights or other architectural elements within the room.

Accents: The resurgence of interest in Retro furniture from Mid-Century industrial designers is appropriate. Combining commercial-type cooking equipment or storage racks (open stainless steel racks) works well—as do functional carts. Curvilinear, soft naturalistic wood furniture in chairs and tables works as well.

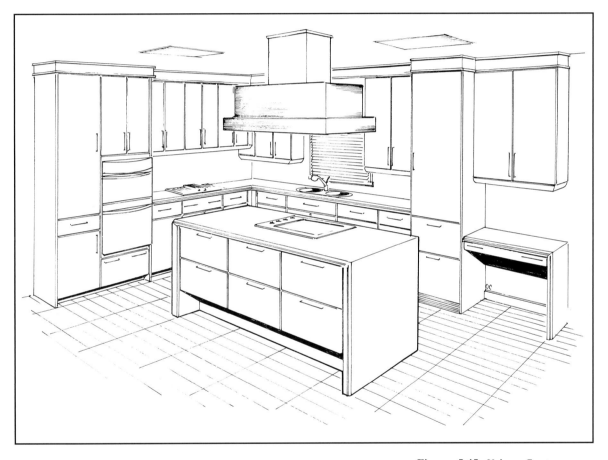

Figure 5.45 *Urban Contemporary Kitchen*
Sleek with repetitive sharp angles, this look relies in part on the strong lines of hardware to make a statement. (Courtesy of Don O'Connor, Wood-Mode Inc.)

Figure 5.46 *Urban Contemporary Kitchen*
The strong sense of sculpted space, simple materials and unique light fixtures create an Urban-inspired kitchen. (Courtesy of Showcase/V6B Design Group, Vancouver, British Columbia)

Figure 5.47 *Urban Contemporary Kitchen*
Translucent doors in a metal frame add to the Urban feel. (Courtesy of Showcase/V6B Design Group, Vancouver, British Columbia)

Figure 5.48 *Urban Contemporary Kitchen*
Sleek glossy surfaces and flat doors, accented by the strong lines of the metal pulls, all contribute to the architectural feel of this space. (Courtesy of NY Loft)

Figure 5.49 *Urban Contemporary Kitchen*
Three strong block shapes define the lineal quality of this restrained contemporary kitchen. (Courtesy of Sub-Zero Freezer Co.)

Figure 5.50 *Urban Contemporary Kitchen*
Sleek acrylic/polyester cabinets are accented by a horizontally placed pull. Note the curved shape of the hood and furniture in the foreground in this Urban styled room. (Courtesy of Sandra L. Steiner-Houck, CKD – Mechanicsburg, Pennsylvania)

Figure 5.51 *Urban Contemporary Bathroom*
Stand-alone cherry cabinets and an oversized fire clay lavatory are combined with Carrara marble. The use of different materials and simple shapes are key elements in this Urban Contemporary bathroom. (Courtesy of American Standard)

Figure 5.52 *Urban Contemporary Kitchen*
Once again, curved shapes with sharp materials are used in this space. The curved hood, ceiling treatment and glass eating top are hard-edged Contemporary materials. Note the formed plywood stools: a furniture piece reminiscent of Mid-Century Modern design. (Courtesy of Erica Westeroth, CKD and co-designers Tim Scott and Virginia Marsh – Toronto, Ontario)

Figure 5.53 *Urban Contemporary Kitchen*
Glossy, sleek cabinetry with minimalist slab doors contrasts with a worn-looking wood floor in this eclectic version of an Urban Contemporary style that emphasizes interesting textures. (Courtesy of KraftMaid Cabinetry)

Figure 5.56 *Mid-Century Modern Kitchen*
Mid-Century design interpreted by the Scandinavian artists
was sleeker and simpler in the materials used. Colors were
more subdued and naturalistic. This kitchen is reminiscent
of such styling with its naturalistic wood tones combined
with stainless steel finishes and glass tile at the backsplash,
peppered with black, lime green and gray color tones.
Reproduction Modern Scandinavian furniture would work
well in this kitchen. (Courtesy of Tim Scott and Erica
Westeroth, CKD – Toronto, Ontario)

Figure 5.57 *Mid-Century Modern Kitchen*
This award-winning kitchen features a fun asymmetrical mix of colors and shapes quite reminiscent of the playfulness of Mid-Century Modernistic design. Curves in the custom veneer work on the side of the island are repeated in circle cut-outs in the steel furniture, as well as in the shape of the island. A mosaic glass tile on the countertop repeats the colors seen in the woodworking. (Melissa Smith, CKD, and Carla Taylor, CKD – Nashville, Tennessee)

Figure 5.58 *Mid-Century Modern Kitchen*
This kitchen was created by mixing reproduction decorative arts throughout this set. Notice the colorful 1950s plastics used in shapes very much in tune with this exuberant time in American history. (Courtesy of Viking Range Corporation)

Figure 5.59 *Mid-Century Modern Kitchen*
This kitchen creates the "retro mood" through the use of the easily changeable decorative surfaces and accessories. Take away the 1950s chrome and vinyl table, Coca Cola sign and abstract tile mural, and this kitchen could easily transition into a sleeker Contemporary setting with its natural maple, deep cobalt-blue wood and floor finishes and stainless steel accents. The room feels retro because of the accessories added from the consumer's collection. (Courtesy of Ellen Cheever, CMKBD, ASID, and Pietro Giorgi, Sr., CMKBD – Wilmington, Delaware)

A CLOSING COMMENT

This detailed discussion of historical data is the way to begin building an understanding of past architectural styles and antiques. Seeing and naming different elements of past artistry helps you differentiate between styles.

When considering how to separate or to match styles with historic collections, remember these styles did not follow one another chronologically. Rather they overlapped as an emerging style, frequently borrowing features from one declining in popularity. Usually, a new style appeared at the top end of the market, while the older continued slowly down to the middle-class. As a designer studying historical architecture might expect, the top of the market was also the first to benefit from the latest technological developments. Oftentimes, individual features of a new style were tacked on to existing dwellings creating transitional forms. Additionally, the three social classes familiar to us today (upper, middle, and working) also emerged as the population changed from a rural community to a predominantly urban one. Therefore, each style of home presents itself in various configurations appropriate for the more ornate upper-class dwellings, a more middle approach and the simplest working man's version.

If all this talk of architectural history seems overwhelming at first, remember this entire discussion is simply a platform. Don't let it limit you by technically defining "what goes with what." Just the opposite —understanding the details of past styles should free you to create new interpretations.

Rather than overcomplicate the definition of a certain theme, focus on the sense of the style. The montage of well thought-out design details defined by the client's preferences is far more interesting—and satisfying—than a room created by slavishly following the rules established by historians.

Design Principles

1.1   An Historical Kitchen. xii
1.2   1940s Kitchen xiii
1.3   1960s Kitchen xiv
1.4   Kitchens from Today – Traditional. xv
1.5   Kitchens from Today – Contemporary xvi
1.6   Historical Plumbing xvii
1.7   Historical Bathroom xviii
1.8   Bathrooms from Today xix

**Chapter 1 – The Basics Of Beauty: Developing
Skill, Expanding Creativity And Appreciating Style**
1.9   The Basics of Beauty 2
1.10 The Basics of Beauty: A Unified Kitchen . . . 5
1.11 The Basics of Beauty: A Unified Bathroom . . . 6
1.12 The Basics of Beauty:
      Highly Stylized Kitchen 8
1.13 The Basics of Beauty: A Timeless Look 9
1.14 The Basics of Beauty:
      Tailored Timeless Design 10

Chapter 3 – The Elements of Design
3.1   Kitchen Featuring Horizontal Lines 16
3.2   Kitchen Featuring Horizontal Lines 17
3.3   Bathroom Featuring Horizontal Lines 18
3.4   Kitchen Featuring Vertical Lines 19
3.5   Bathroom Featuring Vertical Lines. 20
3.6   Kitchen Featuring Curved Lines. 21
3.7   Kitchen Featuring Curved Lines. 22
3.8   Kitchen Featuring Diagonal Lines 24
3.9   Bathroom Featuring Diagonal Lines 25
3.10 Kitchen Designed with Rectangular Shapes. 27
3.11 Home Office Designed with
      Rectangular Shapes. 28
3.12 Kitchen Designed with Square Shapes. 29
3.13 Kitchen Designed with Diagonal or
      Angled Shapes 30
3.14 Bathroom Designed with Diagonal or
      Angled Shapes 31
3.15 Kitchen Designed with Triangular Shapes . . 32
3.16 Kitchen Designed with Curved or
      Circular Shapes. 33

3.17 Bathroom Designed with Curved or
      Circular Shapes. 34
3.18 Kitchen with Structural Pattern 36
3.19 Bathroom with Structural Pattern 37
3.20 Kitchen with Naturalistic Pattern 38
3.21 Bathroom with Naturalistic Pattern 39
3.22 Kitchen with Stylized Pattern. 40
3.23 Bathroom with Stylized Pattern 41
3.24 Kitchen with Geometric Pattern 42
3.25 Bathroom with Geometric Pattern 43
3.26 Kitchen with Abstract Pattern. 44
3.27 Bathroom with Abstract Pattern 45
3.28 Create a Pyramid. 47
3.29 Create an "H" Form 48
3.30 Create a Step Ladder. 49
3.31 Kitchen with Rugged Textures 51
3.32 Kitchen with Smooth Textures 52
3.33 Kitchen Combining Textures 53
3.34 Contemporary Bathroom Combining
      Smooth and Rugged Textures. 54
3.41 Kitchen with Monochromatic
      Color Scheme 63
3.42 Bathroom with Monochromatic
      Color Scheme 64
3.43 Bath with Analogous Color Scheme. 65
3.44 Kitchen with Analogous and
      Complementary Accent Color Scheme. 66
3.45 Triad Color Scheme 67
3.46 Complementary Color Scheme. 68
3.47 Complementary Color Scheme. 69
3.48 Neutral Color Scheme. 70
3.49 Neutral Color Scheme. 71

Chapter 4 – The Principles of Design
4.2   Kitchen Designed with
      Symmetrical Balance 78
4.3   Bathroom Designed with
      Symmetrical Balance 79
4.4   Kitchen Designed with
      Asymmetrical Balance 80
4.5   Kitchen Designed with
      Asymmetrical Balance 81

4.6   Bathroom Designed with
        Asymmetrical Balance 82
4.7   Kitchen Designed with Radial Balance 83
4.9   Rhythm Created by Repetitious Design 85
4.10   Rhythm Created by Repetitious Design 86
4.12   Rhythm Created by Alternating Design 88
4.13   Rhythm Created by Alternating Design 89
4.15   Rhythm Created by Progressive Design 91
4.16   Rhythm Created by Progressive Design 92
4.17   Area Emphasis 94
4.18   Area Emphasis 95
4.19   Area Emphasis 96
4.20   Area Emphasis 97
4.21   Theme Emphasis 98
4.22   Theme Emphasis 99

Chapter 5 – Creating a Theme Environment
5.2   American Country Potting Room 111
5.3   American Colonial Kitchen 112
5.5   Shaker Kitchen 115
5.8   Arts & Crafts Kitchen 120
5.9   Southwestern Dining Room Setting 122
5.10   Spanish Mission Kitchen 123
5.12   American Georgian Cabinet 126
5.13   American Georgian Bathroom 127
5.15   Federal Kitchen 130
5.16   Federal Butler's Pantry 131
5.18   Victorian Kitchen 134
5.19   Victorian Bathroom 135
5.21   English Country Kitchen 139

5.22   English Country Kitchen 140
5.25   French Country Kitchen 145
5.26   French Country Vanity 146
5.28   Italian Tuscan Kitchen 149
5.29   Italian Tuscan Kitchen 150
5.31   Biedermeier-styled Entertainment Center . . 154
5.32   Biedermeier-styled Bathroom 155
5.34   Artisan Crafted Kitchen 160
5.35   Artisan Crafted Vanity Area 161
5.36   Artisan Crafted Kitchen 162
5.37   Artisan Crafted Kitchen 163
5.38   Artisan Crafted Bathroom 164
5.39   Artisan Crafted Bathroom 165
5.41   Pacific Rim Kitchen 168
5.42   East Meets West Bathroom 169
5.43   East Meets West Bathroom 170
5.44   East Meets West Bathroom 171
5.46   Urban Contemporary Kitchen 174
5.47   Urban Contemporary Kitchen 175
5.48   Urban Contemporary Kitchen 176
5.49   Urban Contemporary Kitchen 177
5.50   Urban Contemporary Kitchen 178
5.51   Urban Contemporary Bathroom 179
5.52   Urban Contemporary Kitchen 180
5.53   Urban Contemporary Kitchen 181
5.55   Mid-Century Modern Kitchen 185
5.56   Mid-Century Modern Kitchen 186
5.57   Mid-Century Modern Kitchen 187
5.58   Mid-Century Modern Kitchen 188
5.59   Mid-Century Modern Kitchen 189

Chapter 3 – The Elements of Design

3.35   The Color Wheel 56

3.36   The Three Categories of Hues
        on the Color Wheel .58

3.37   Chroma Scale for the Color Yellow 59

3.38   Value Scale 60

3.39   Three-dimensional Color Wheel
        Reflecting Each Hue's Chroma and Value . .61

3.40   Graphically Understanding
        Color Harmonies 62

Chapter 4 – The Principles of Design

4.1   A Diagram of Symmetrical and
        Asymmetrical Balance 77

4.8   Diagram of Repetitive Rhythm 84

4.11   A Diagram of Alternating Rhythm 87

4.14   A Diagram of Progressive Rhythm 90

Chapter 5 – Creating a Theme Environment

5.1   American Colonial Kitchen 110

5.4   Shaker Kitchen 114

5.6   Arts & Crafts Kitchen 118

5.7   Prairie School Kitchen 119

5.11   American Georgian Kitchen 125

5.14   Federal Kitchen 129

5.17   Victorian Kitchen .133

5.20   English Country Kitchen 138

5.23   French Country Kitchen 143

5.24   French Country Kitchen 144

5.27   Italian Tuscan Kitchen 148

5.30   Biedermeier Kitchen 153

5.33   Artisan-Inspired Kitchen
        That Includes Art Deco Details 159

5.40   Pacific Rim Kitchen 167

5.45   Urban Contemporary Kitchen 173

5.54   Retro Contemporary Kitchen:
        Mid-Century Modern 184

INDEX

Aalto, Alvar **182**

Abstract pattern **35, 44-45**

Actual texture **50**

Adams, Beverly **8, 9**

Alig, Beverly A. **185**

Alternating rhythm **87-89**

American Classic Formal style **108, 124-135**

American Classic Rustic style **108-123**

American Standard, Inc. **170, 179**

American Traditional style **109-114**

American Woodmark **16, 51**

Analogous colors **62, 65-66**

Applegate, Vernon **18, 89**

Architectural history review **104-107**

Area emphasis **93-97**

Art Deco **106, 158-159**

Art Nouveau **106, 117**

Artisan crafted styles **156, 158-165**

Arts & Crafts style **106, 116-120, 156, 158, 165**

Asian Pacific theme (see East meets West)

Asian theme **107**

Asymmetrical balance **76-77, 80-82, 168**

Balance **76-83**

Balint, Jacqueline **165, 171**

Barragan, Luis **107**

Bates, Susan **30**

Bauhaus School of Design **106**

Biedermeier styling **106, 152-155**

Blue **72**

Bohn, Laura **82**

Bordwin, Andrew **54**

Boriack, Nancy L. **40**

Bowden, Jere **131**

Brewer, Marcel **182**

Brown **73**

Budget **11, 12**

Butler's pantry **131**

Carroll, Laurie **45**

Cheever, Ellen **42, 44, 47, 88, 130, 189**

Cheng, Fu-Tung **17, 168**

Chippendale **124**

Chroma **59**

Ciccarello, Gerard **80**

Classicism **104-105**

Client questions **11, 12, 13**

Client relationship **12, 13, 14**

Collector's mix **104**

Colonial style **xii, 109-110, 112**

Color **15, 55-75**

Color attributes **59**

Color categories **56**

Color harmony **62**

Color intensity (chroma) **59**

Color value **60**

Color wheel **56, 58, 61**

Complementary colors **62, 68-69**

Construction **13**

Consumers **xi**

Contemporary style **xiv, 102-103, 107-108, 156-189**

Continuity **84**

Cook, Charles S. **64**

Corsi Cabinet Co. **112**

Country style **102, 109-111**

Creativity **3-4**

Curved lines (bath) **21**

Curved lines (kitchen) **22**

Curved or circular shape **26, 33-34**

Deane, Peter **xv**

Decora Cabinets **134**

Deras, Peggy **145**

Diagonal lines (bath) **25**

Diagonal lines (kitchen) **24**

Diagonal or angled shape **26, 30-31**

Dilger, Heather **134**

Dixion, Joyce **28**

Documentation **14**

Domination **93**

Donohue, Kathleen **3**

Downsview Kitchens **5**

Drenckhahn, Michelle **25**

Dulacki, Catherine **122**

Dura Supreme **19**

Eames, Charles and Ray **157, 182**

Early American style **105**

East meets West styles **156, 166-171**

Eclectic style **102-103**

Eclectic Transitional **107**

Edwards, Karen **52**

Egyptian motif **106, 152**

Elements of design **15**

Emphasis **93-100**

English Country style **136-140**

Entertainment center **154**

Euro look, **156**

European Classic Formal style **108, 152-155**

European Classic Rustic style **108, 136-150**

Ewing, Rebecca **72-73**

Fakhoury, George **xvi**

Falke, Larry A. **165, 171**

Farrell, Rick, **63**

Federal style **128-131**

Fife, Duncan **128**

Flock, Frederick A. **78**

Fly, Gay **155**

Foreman, Diane **43, 79**

Form **15, 46-49**

French Country style **141-146**

French Empire style **152-153**

French Provincial **141**

Fulton, Jeannie **127, 163**

Gargano, Martha **34**

Geometric pattern **35, 42-43**

Georgian style **124-127**

Gilmer, Jennifer **120, 154**

Giorgi, Sr., Pietro **44, 47, 88, 189**

Giuliani, Tess **69, 98**

Good design **xi, 3, 4, 7**

Gool, Pete **36**

Gothic **105**

Graves, Michael **107**

Great room **xv**

Green **72**

Gustafson, Ron **32**

"H" Form **46, 48**

Hadley Photography **40**

Halajian, Arthur Krikor **6**

Hathaway, Kaye **67**

Hendricks, Jerry **85**

Hepplewhite **124**

Heritage Custom Cabinetry **146**

Hessinger, Paulette **36**

High-tech look **156**

Hilsabeck, Jr., Alan **169**

History **xi-xvi** (kitchen), **xvii-xix** (bath)

Home office **28**

Horizontal line (bath) **18**

Horizontal line (kitchen) **16, 17**

Hower, Bob **134**

Huber, Timothy **53**

Hue **55, 56, 58**

Hunt, Judy Adams **48**

Idea book **13**

International School of Architecture **106**

Jacuzzi **65**

Kalisch, Rochelle, **27**

Kaskel Architectural Photography **92, 97**

Keys, Diana Wogulis **86**

King Tut **106**

Kitchen & Bath Systems **13**

Kitchen history, **xi-xvi**

Kitchen Planning, Residential Construction **13**

Kohler Co. **xiii, xvii, xviii, 2** (Design Center) **82**

Koran, Leonard **166**

KraftMaid Cabinetry **96, 181**

Kranz, Raymond **123**

Larsen, Debbie **33**

Leach, Bernadine **145**

Leach, Peter **38, 126**

Lenner, Daniel **21**

Levine, Steven M. **54**

Lieberknecht, Eric **10**

Line **15-26**

Livingston, David **86, 145, 164**

Lodge style **121-122**

Margonelli, Peter **52**

Marsh, Virginia **180**

Mauro, Patricia **150**

McClain Imagery **44, 47, 88**

McEvoy, Maura, **27**

McFadden, Dan **33**

McLain, Linda **66**

Metropolitan Museum of Art **xviii**

Mid-Century Modern style **10, 102, 106, 156, 182-189**

Millman, Matthew **17, 168**

Millman, Robert **112**

Modern bath **xix**

Monochromatic colors **63-64**

Motif **102**

Narod, Bob **120**

National Kitchen & Bath Association **11, 13**

Naturalistic pattern **35, 38-39**

Neutra, Richard **182**

Neutral color scheme **70-71**

1920s-30s bath **xvii-xviii**

1940s kitchen **xiii**

1960s kitchen **xiv**

1970s kitchen **xv**

19th century architecture **105**

Noguchi, Isamu **182**

NY Loft **176**

O'Connor, Don **110, 114, 118, 119, 125, 129, 133, 136, 138, 143, 144, 148, 153, 159, 167, 173, 184**

Old World style **xv, 8, 94, 102, 107**

Orange **73**

Pattern **35-45**

Peacock, Christopher **140**

Pearse, Don **139**

Period **102**

Personalizing design **11**

Picasso, Pablo **4**

Pink **73**

Post-modernism **107**

Potting room **111**

Power, Sally **161**

Prairie School kitchen **119**

Primary hues **57-58**

Principles of design **1, 5, 15, 76-100**

Product specifications **13**

Professional Resource Library **xi**

Program phase **11**

Progressive rhythm **90-92**

Purple **73**

Pyramid **46-47**

Queen Victoria **132**

Radial balance **76, 83**

Rawson, Greg **xix**

Rectangular shape **26-28**

Red **73**

Reese, Susan **83**

Reiss, Bryan **xv**

Renaissance **105**

Reniers, Rusty **6**

Repetitive rhythm **84-86**

Retro style **106, 156, 173, 182-184**

Rhythm **76, 84-92**

Rustic Americana **121-123**

Rutt HandCrafted Cabinetry **22, 139**

Rymwid, Peter **xvi, 163**

Saarinen, Eero **182**

Salerno, Peter Ross **28, 39, 71, 135**

Salerno, Tracy Ann **71**

Scandinavian Country style **151**

Scandinavian style **182, 186**

Sciascia, Karen **34**

Scott, Tim **20, 24, 180, 186**

Seals, Susan **85**

Secondary hues **57-58**

Shaker style **113-115, 158**

Shamaniam, Oscar **2**

Shane, Madelane **21**

Shape **15, 26-34**

Shaw, George Bernard **4**

Sheraton **124**

Showcase/V6B Design Group **94-95, 174-175**

Showrooms **3**

Signature element **104**

Smith, Melissa **187**

Smith, Michael **49**

Society of Preservation of New England Antiques **xii**

Southwestern style **107**

Space **15, 46-49**

Spanish Mission style **121-123**

Square shape **26, 29**

Staal, Beverly **37, 99**

Steiner-Houck, Sandra L. **41, 178**

Step ladder **46, 49**

Stewart, Kelly **xv**

Stickley, Gustav **106**

Stillman, Michael **122**

Stoner, Julie A. **31**

Structural pattern **35-37**

Stultz, Scott **xv**

Style **1, 3, 101, 190**

Stylized pattern **35, 40-41**

Sub-Zero Freezer Co. **130, 177**

Sullivan, Sally Ann **149**

Survey **11-14**

Symmetrical balance **76-79**

Taste **3**

Taylor, Carla **187**

Taylor, Michael **106-107**

Tertiary hues **57-58**

Texture **15, 50-54**

Theme emphasis **98-99**

Theme environment **101-189**

Theme style terminology **102**

Thompson, Craig **68**

Thompson, Marie A. **164**

Tilander, Sheila **91**

Timeless look/design **7, 8, 9, 10, 99**

Traditional style **xv, 102, 109-155**

Tran, Gioi Ngoc **18, 29, 89**

Transforming space with color **74-75**

Transitional style **9, 102, 107**

Triad colors **62, 67**

Triangular shape **26, 32**

Trzcinski, Tom **68**

Turk, Roger **37, 79**

Tuscan style **107, 147-150**

21st century design **156-189**

Umberger, John **10, 131**

Unfitted kitchen **xv**

Unified look **4, 5, 6**

Unity of design **4, 5, 6**

Urban Contemporary styles **156-157, 172-181, 185**

Valentine, Diana **86**

Vernacular **103**

Vertical line (bath) **20**

Vertical line (kitchen) **19**

Victorian **105, 132-135**

Viking Range Corp. **188**

Visual texture **50**

Vitale, Peter **81**

Wabi-Sabi—for Artists, Designers, Poets & Philosophers **166**

Weinstein, Lonne **54**

Westeroth, Erica, **20, 24, 180,186**

White, Mark **97**

Williams, Karen **38, 126**

Winterthur Museum **130**

Wm Ohs Inc. **149**

Wood-Mode Inc. **xiv, 32, 70, 81, 110, 111, 114, 115, 118, 119, 125, 129, 133, 136, 138, 143, 144, 148, 153, 159, 160, 162, 167, 173, 184**

World War II **106**

Wright, Frank Lloyd **106**

Wright, Russel **182, 183**

Yang, Wendy **92**

Yankelovich survey **75**

Yellow **72**